Praise for Oliver Sheppard's *Destruction: Text I*:

"Given the chance, Sheppard will lead you down dark and unfamiliar paths, to moments of weird beauty.... Reading Sheppard's poetry is a little like listening to a conversation between Nietzsche and William Blake during a showing of Peckinpah's *Cross of Iron*. Using a wide range of forms and cultural references, Sheppard illustrates the human condition in ways that take as much account of its absence as its presence."

—John Foster, *A Thousand Trivialities*

———

"These poems tell stories--of hell, destruction, death, life, family, to personal memoir. Oliver Sheppard's book of poetry, *Destruction: Text I*, will appeal to readers whose literary interests span across multiple genres such as mythology, astronomy, the theological, and especially the philosophical and metaphysical. The poems are highly intertextual, connecting to scientific texts (some obscure), sacred text (some esoteric), and a variety of other inspirational sources. It reminds me of the way T.S. Eliot weaves in both the ancient and modern into his own free verse, in the longer poems."

—Peggy Semingson, University of Texas

Order *Destruction: Text I* now on Amazon or at ikonographpress.com

Thirteen Nocturnes

by Oliver Sheppard

Ikonograph Press   -   Dallas, Texas

Death and the Maiden (detail), by George Clark Stanton (1870)

Thirteen Nocturnes

by Oliver Sheppard

Ikonograph Press - *Dallas, Texas*

Thirteen Nocturnes

All formatting, layout, design, and typesetting are copyright © 2018 by Ikonograph Press.

ISSUED June, 2018 by Ikonograph Press, PO Box 140551, Dallas, Texas 75214

Design: Anne Hedonia and anonymous. All source images used in *Thirteen Nocturnes* were created before 1923 and/or are in the public domain. Images have been modified to appear in this book.

Library of Congress Cataloging-in-Publication data available upon request.

ISBN-13: 978-1978331204
ISBN-10: 1978331207

Edition 1 of 4

THIRTEEN NOCTURNES

TABLE OF CONTENTS

FOREWORD

by John Foster

It takes guts to write and publish a book of poetry at this point in the history of the world. This has little to do with Theodor Adorno's comment about the barbarism of writing poetry in the wake of Auschwitz (I think he was talking about lyric poetry, and in any case he backed off it later). No, the real problem with pursuing the poetic form at the current moment is the fundamental absurdity of the modern.

Historically, poetry has involved the creative use of language to write with greater depth (or with greater precision) than that available in the medium of prose. In the spectacular society in which we live, the depths beneath the surface have evaporated and precision, more often than not, is simply a matter of giving the right name to the right specter.

Oliver Sheppard's poetry strives mightily against the bonds of the age. His pieces in *Destruction: Text I*, his first collection of verse, did not, unlike so many exemplars of modern poetry, exhaust their energies in parsing the minutiae of human internality. In that book, Sheppard's writings were distinctly external in their focus, ranging widely from the mechanized battlefields of the Second World War's Eastern Front to the event horizons of collapsing stars. This may strike one as thinking big in a way that strains the bonds of coherent conception, but Sheppard's pieces are united in the consistency of a dark atmosphere that creates a space for the examination of human and trans- (or perhaps super-) human experience.

Sheppard's poetry is, so far as I am aware, something of a change of mode for him. I will offer as a caveat that we know each other in that via-the-internet sort of way that is common for people whose subcultural attachments overlap. I can't remember whether his work first came to my attention because he published at Souciant.com (for which I am also a contributor) or whether I only found out about that later. But I do know a few verifiable facts. Oliver Sheppard is simply the most passionate fan of Killing Joke that I have ever met. He also follows deathrock with the same sort of obsessive passion that I have for European hardcore punk. Where I would be talking about Pandemonium's *Wir fahren gegen Dreck* he can discourse at length about Fliehende Stürme's *An den Ufern.*

Perhaps it is this virtuoso level familiarity with the obscure that first interested me in his work. In pieces for Cvlt Nation or (more occasionally) Bandcamp, Sheppard gives his readers access to a pool of knowledge that is as broad as it is deep. What seems to pull it all together is a dark, although not to say morbid, aesthetic.

Given the chance, Sheppard will lead you down dark and unfamiliar paths, to moments of weird beauty.

Reading Sheppard's poetry is a little like listening to a conversation between Nietzsche and William Blake during a showing of Peckinpah's *Cross of Iron*. Using a wide range of forms and cultural references, Sheppard illustrates the human condition in ways that take as much account of its absence as its presence. Thus we find early in a cycle of Second World War-themed pieces, the following:

> Severe grey angles
> Turretless malevolence
> Squat steel gunned bulwark

It takes a certain kind of audacity to compose a cycle of haikus about war on the Eastern Front, but it is precisely this breadth of conception that lifts Sheppard's poetry above the mean. His poetry seems fascinated with the human, but also with the superhuman, with the action of entities at the far ends of space or, as in his references to Persephone, descending into the underworld. In a piece entitled "Achromatic #1" Sheppard writes:

> A hyperdimensional SPHERE of battleship gray
> Lays some distance southwestward of its
> RECTANGULAR and TRAPEZOIDAL cousins

The terms and mode of expression are stark, recalling Pound's quotations from the letters of the vorticist sculptor Henri Gaudier-Brzeska before the latter's death in battle in 1915. Indeed, Sheppard's writing in Destruction: Text I is redolent of the desperate modernism of the interwar period, inflected through the lens of late 20th underground culture. His mix of longer and shorter pieces and quotations from other authors (both in epigrams and longer elements) gives the feel of Hannah Höch's collages, but with a later 20th century atmosphere in which playfulness has been replaced by an ineluctable consciousness of the gigantic and of the finitude of things.

In Oliver Sheppard's poetry there are moments in which it appears that the fabric of reality is coming apart at the seams, held together only tenuously by the images that mediate human social relations. Sheppard's darkly beautiful verse investigates the dark interstices of this system of images, looking both below and beyond to stark and often threatening realities. Often the human is absent, but it is reconstituted and reflected into this emptiness, leaving the afterimage of an unsettling universe. If there is a barbaric dimension to this writing it is a barbarism that, in a certain sense, works to recover the human.

—John Foster
Portland, OR
A Thousand Trivialities

PREFACE

In Hans Henny Jahnn's novella "The Night of Lead" (printed most recently in the excellent Atlas Press collection *The Living Are Few, the Dead Are Many*), the protagonist, Matthieu, finds himself trapped in a nightmare city that could have easily served as the setting of a German Expressionist silent film. As the story progresses, Matthieu seeks solace in one of the nameless city's dour bars. A weighty conversation ensues with a barmaid; she tells Matthieu:

> In the depths of the night one knows nothing of the day. It is expected, but the time will come when we will never greet the dawn again... One day the turbines which generate our light will come to a standstill, break down, or show their will in some other fashion. Water is also not in man's control, but part of a larger time than man.

The barmaid adds: "All who believe in the patience of creation will be surprised by its violence." Decades after Jahnn's work, Cormac McCarthy took up similar apocalyptic themes in *Blood Meridian:* "The way of the world is to bloom and to flower and die but in the affairs of men there is no waning and the noon of his expression signals the onset of night"—or so opines the malevolent Judge. In the century before either Jahnn or McCarthy wrote their works, Lord Byron penned "Darkness" along similar lines:

> I had a dream, which was not all a dream.
> The bright sun was extinguish'd, and the stars
> Did wander darkling in the eternal space,
> Rayless, and pathless, and the icy earth
> Swung blind and blackening in the moonless air

Byron's "Darkness," Jahnn's "The Night of Lead," and Cormac McCarthy's *Blood Meridian* (and especially his *The Road*) touch upon the theme of darkness—but especially *night*—as coeval with apocalypse. This leitmotif in Western literature stretches all the way back to the Bible, as when the prophet Joel proclaimed in the 5th century BCE, "The sun will be turned to darkness" or when Matthew announced, five centuries later, "The sun shall be darkened" in the time of the eschaton. Similar examples run throughout the Bible, and eventually throughout all Western literature, in instances too numerous to mention.

This tradition has existed uneasily with another Western tradition, a kind of counter-tradition, rooted in Greece, where night, far from being day's counterpoint, was seen as its birth-mother. And so there is Hesiod's *Theogony*, which in the 7th century BCE stated: "Out of Chaos came Darkness and black Night, and out of Night came Light and Day, her children conceived after union in love with Darkness." The idea of night as the mother (rather than the opposing principle) of day resonates with the original notion of *apocalypse* as not an example of gloom but of epiphanic revelation: of light-bringing. The confusion of this notion of apocalypse (that is, revelatory unveiling, or illumination) with gloomy darkness was a later development, just as Lucifer's original aspect as lightbringer was later confused with that of Satanic blackness.

I bring up these points to underscore a key concern of mine when I composed *Thirteen Nocturnes.* As I was writing *Destruction: Text I* last year, I thought very much about "the world made black as pitch" (a line from my poem in this volume, "Nocturne No. 1.") and in a very simple, obvious way it struck me that we fall into darkness all the time—that is, night; that which befalls the part of the earth that rotates to face away from the sun. This is a kind of daily practice-run for when "the time will come when we will never greet the dawn again," to quote Jahnn. I used this simple idea as a springboard for subsequent meditations, and they resulted in this book.

Most of the poems in *Thirteen Nocturnes* were written over an eight month period, from late 2017 into the spring of 2018. For me this was a period of not-inconsequential introspection, self-examination, and even of sustained sobriety. Hopefully the poems in this book reflect only two of these things.

Excluding things like chapter heading pages, this book is comprised of about 200 pages of poetry. To get it down to this length I had to excise about 70 pages of poems that either did not fit the theme of this work or measure up in some other way. The idea of an unwieldy 300+ page book of poetry did not appeal to me. The excised poems may appear in future editions, or in a different book altogether.

And despite what I've written above, I'm not a huge fan of verse whose enjoyment requires a lot of exposition or context. When you think of poems you have enjoyed the most, chances are they are poems that, like Poe's "The Raven," or Whitman's "Song of Myself," do not require much additional explanation for enjoyment. This is not to say that additional explanation cannot enrich enjoyment later. But I'd like to let the poems of *Thirteen Nocturnes* speak for themselves.

I did arrange the pieces in this book according to a certain narrative design, and it is because of this that I feel it is important to insist that *Thirteen Nocturnes* be read sequentially, from front to back, each poem in its order. *Thirteen Nocturnes* is not meant to be dipped into selectively. Maybe this seems counterintuitive to readers used to anthologies of poetry; but neither is this an anthology. *Thirteen Nocturnes* is, in the end, a narrative work, and I hope readers can afford me the generosity of treating it as such.

My constant reading companions during the writing of *Thirteen Nocturnes* were Giacomo Leopardi, Cormac McCarthy, Robert Penn Warren, William Blake, and Georg Trakl. My listening companions were Hector Berlioz, Killing Joke, Musta Paraati, Son House, and Rudimentary Peni. I tried to avoid watching too much of the daily depressing news cycle about Donald Trump while writing this book. Other than that, I did not go very far out of my way to avoid the macabre. Clive Barker and Thomas Ligotti were never far from my nightstand.

There are some people that deserve acknowledgement here. Per Nilsson, Philosopher and Senior Lecturer at the Academy of Fine Arts at Umeå University in Sweden, and author of the excellent *Non Serviam*, is due credit for his enthusiastic support of my first book. Peggy Semingson at the University of Texas has also been a great supporter from early on. Jack Control of World Burns to Death (and Severed Head of State, Butcher, and Enormous Door Mastering) has been an important source of feedback in the development of this work. Thanks are owed to Davey Bales of The Wraith and Lost Tribe (and Davey is himself a fellow poet of no mean talent). Special thanks are also due fellow Texas poet Heather Blank, whose excellent volume *Charcoal Cocktails* was the direct impetus for my putting together last year's *Destruction: Text I*. My mom, Theresa, without whose encouragement none of this would have been possible, deserves recognition; and the same goes for the love of my life, Sara Hawkins, whose support was critical to the completion of *Thirteen Nocturnes*. Thanks are owed to Erin and Katrin Powell of Awen for their friendship. Gary Evans came to the rescue with a replacement hard drive when an early draft of *Thirteen Nocturnes* was, I thought, lost in a computer crash. A big thank you to Bossy Boots, the feral cat, for his constant, muse-like inspiration. And thanks to editor James Olivard for providing the copy on the back of this book. Thanks are owed to many of my friends and family in the DIY punk, hardcore punk, postpunk, and deathrock communities. (They have been the main purchasers of my books so far!)

And, more solemnly—last, but not least, to the departed: My grandparents Oliver and Shirley DeLong; Barbara Hawkins; and Shawn Terry of Guilty Strangers. All of them are gone far too soon. *Eheu fugaces labuntur anni...*

—Oliver Sheppard
Dallas, TX
June, 2018

Dedication

These nocturnal lines are dedicated
To all beautiful things that have
Been brought about through
Terrible means: *For
There is much that is marvelous
That is wicked.*

—O.S.

"The day is done, and the darkness
        Falls from the wings of Night."

—Henry Wadsworth Longfellow,
    "The Day is Done" (1844)

"Somewhere the sun shines in the east."

—Killing Joke, "A New Day" (1984)

PROLOGUE

MY HEART, WITHOUT REASON

And o'er his heart, a shadow
—POE

My heart, without reason, is singing—
My mind, without burning, is fire—
My thoughts, without friction, are racing
To comprehend infinite fire,
To comprehend infinite fire.

My soul is aloft far above me—
My body's asleep; and, what's more,
I nurse an old darkness inside me
For such is the heart at its core,
For such is the heart at its core.

I tend an old darkness inside me
And maybe I will ever more.

My heart, without reason, is singing—
My mind, without burning, is fire—
My thoughts, they are always attempting
To comprehend infinite fire,
To comprehend infinite fire.

"Those of us who carry in our chests these carrion hearts"

WE, THE CARRION HEARTED

Je suis un cimetière abhorré de la lune
—BAUDELAIRE

My heart is like roadkill,
Mashed up into bloody clumps,
Run over and scattered—
A red flourish on the wayside.
Pieces of it litter crossroads.

Others know they've struck it;
But it is, after all, roadkill.
They move on.

Roadkill is food for some animals,
For nature's profligate opportunists,
For hunters of the dead and the dying.
For some, it's a dietary staple.

(Like you, O *corvus corone*,
Austere and funerary omen!
And yet—you whose taste
Is for dead meat that
Stinks like carrion flowers—
Even to you would I say, "Feast well,
Deathbird!")

Those of us who carry in
Our chests
These carrion hearts—
We, the carrion-hearted—
Know how well our dead organs
Might be supped,
How too easily they can
Become portions
In others' gruesome diets.

Thirteen Nocturnes

NOCTURNE No. 1

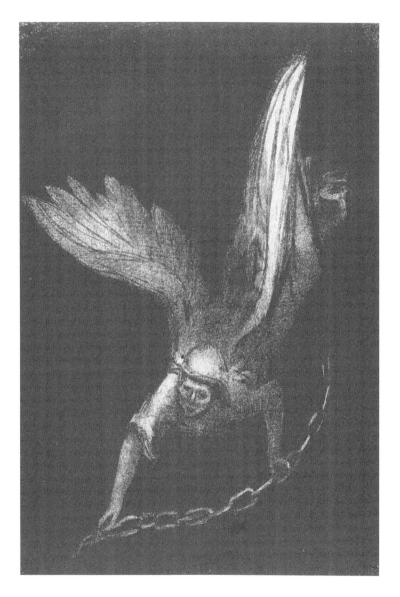

"*Look up!* came a voice. Something opened back the heavens"

NOCTURNE No. 1

> Ibant obscuri, sola sub nocte, per umbram
> Perque domos Ditis vacuas, et inania regna
> —VIRGIL

Look up! came a voice.

Something opened back the heavens
To reveal the monstrous dark that lies behind
Them and which was before them.

Not just the sun—
As in the Revelation to John after
The sixth seal was broken by the Lamb—
But the entire sky
Had become black like sack cloth of goat hair.
The apocalypse of night
Had made its diurnal return, reminding
That worldly darkness recurs
Not only during end-times, but
With scientific precision, routinely—
That earth, in fact, is thrown into
Darkness as a matter of normal course.
The world made black as pitch:
Not a rarity, but quotidian—
Literally a nightly occurrence.

In purple mourning shades, night
Spreads over the planet like
A suppurating wound, a bruising of the sky
Into ever-darker shades of blue, in mottled
        blue-and-violet violence,
Once vibrant but drowned in murky watercolor hues

And then blackened to final blackness,
A shining blackness like flesh slick with
Rot of decay, glut of death; beautifully black
Like a window onto deep space—
Onto the void itself, which is
What night is.

The all-consuming black fire of the night
Drowns the flesh with its chill,
And its bright blackness blinds.
Before it, shadows clamor.

The darkening dome of dusk
Calls out for the
Hidden side of things to
Manifest.

NOCTURNE No. 2

NOCTURNE No. 2

Night was my vigil; I sat it alone,
A nighttime of years never-ending,
Years by myself where light was unknown,
The darkness severe and unbending.
I came upon means in my decades-long fight
To only but briefly relieve it,
And in certain moments I thought I'd found light
But I was a fool to believe it.

NOCTURNE No. 3

"I did what the books on ceremonial magick said"

NOCTURNE No. 3

> La noche, pienso el silencio. La noche emerge de la muerte. La noche
> emerge de la vida. En la noche viven lost faltos de todo.
> —ALEJANDRA PIZARNIK, "La Noche, El Poema" (1971)

I did what the books on ceremonial magick said:
I drew the circle, I assembled
The ingredients (in my shitty apartment),
And I read the chants.
I read them earnestly.
I did this at the right hour—
I did it all at night.

I waited for the spirit of the summoning.
It never came.

I tried this process again, and again.
I was in my teens. I bought the books—
At that time you could only find them
In actual bookstores, brick and mortar.

Maybe that was the problem.
Maybe I didn't have the right books.
Nothing happened.
Absolutely nothing.

Finally, in the early 'oughts
I found the book I thought
I had been missing; I found it online—
A book on ceremonial and

Ritual magick, long out of print.
I ordered it and
Tried everything again, a full
Fifteen years later.

I was thirty years old by this point.

And it worked.
Finally.

The demon I wanted came to me.

NOCTURNE No. 4

NOCTURNE No. 4

A beauty in the darkness lies
For those that go with open heart;
And shadows cannot blind those eyes
For whom the darkness is a part.
Like roses grown on gravestones wild
Illuminated in the gloom
The dark is home to nighttime's child
And midnight is her constant groom.

NOCTURNE No. 5

"The starry rose-petaled demon gave me his name and his seal"

NOCTURNE No. 5

The Martyrium of Night

Last night time's nightmare:
The starry rose-petaled demon
Ran his fingers along my skin,
Slicing me open to the world.
Red carnations fell from my veins;
I was accompanied by twilight.

I was accompanied by twilight
And a shadow lengthened
From my body.
(It became a black moon.)

Cities drifted in the red air
As dust motes dancing in
Shafts of starlight. A
Gilded black sun veined with
Silver was ripped from my chest.

The starry rose-petaled demon
Gave me his name and his seal
And fell forever, dead, in
A cathedral vortex of fire.

"The starry rose-petaled demon
Ran his fingers along my skin,
Slicing me open to the world.
Red carnations fell from my
veins."

—from "Nocturne No. 5," page 51

Intermezzo

"the sickness of the being vomits a black sun of spit"

—Georges Bataille, "Oh Cranium..."

"If the hero in you is slain, then the sun of the depths rises in you, glowing from afar, and from a dreadful place. But all the same, everything that up till now seemed to be dead in you will come to life, and will change into poisonous serpents that will cover the sun, and you will fall into night and confusion."

—C.G. Jung, "Liber Primus" (1915)

Comme tu me plairais, ô nuit! Sans ces étoiles
Dont la lumière parle un langage connu!
Car je cherche le vide, et le noir, et le nu!

—Charles Baudelaire, "Obsession" (1857)

"Unholy activity consumes the heavenly descent of Night. ... Apportioned to the Light was its time, but timeless and spaceless is the Night's dominion."

—Novalis, "Hymns to the Night" (trans. by
Charles E. Passage) (1800)

NOCTURNE No. 6

NOCTURNE No. 6

Beneath the night gale swayed
Flowers, like the sea,
Whose colors are displayed
To eyes that cannot see—
Their beauty all but hidden
By the absence of the sun,
Their petals torn and shredded
By the wind's vague eidolon.
They sit in endless silence,
Now reposed in lifeless sleep,
While a phantom, gently swirling,
Floats upon the deep.

NOCTURNE No. 7

"Sometimes I think that, like my father, I'm a ghost"

NOCTURNE No. 7

Sometimes I think that, like my father,
I'm a ghost: Someone never there
When it matters
Yet felt in awful ways nonetheless
(Also like a ghost; or
Perhaps, even more,
Like a poltergeist).

Will Ouija boards be able to reach me
When I'm gone?
And of the world—have I made
Any sort of impression?
Or on others? (And is it only vanity to wonder this?)
You: Who art thou?
Are you an "alcohol friend,"
Or are you a real friend?
(And who is a real friend to a poet?)

Or aren't we all ghosts—
All of us phantoms, in our
Own way? Haunting reality through the
Nights and days that checker
Our life's calendars, revisiting
Familiar places, out of habit or out of wont.

The night can remind me how we
Can all disappear into blackness
When we want, or when we must.

The dark of the night, you could
Say, is a true friend, if ever
A true friend there was.

You could also say—that
Night surrounds us all like death.

Have you heard the lullaby
That goes, "Oh, beautiful child,
When you were a babe
And I loved you, your eyes
Gave me kisses, and your sighs
Made me breathless...
Oh, beautiful child,
You were my son, and I
Adored you. Your smiles
Were birthday cake wishes,
And they made me breathless.
But now you are gone,
And I'm a mother all alone,
A mother all alone"?

NOCTURNE No. 8

NOCTURNE No. 8

Passages in Parallel

Night gives birth
To peaceful Death;
And love of light of day,
Along with daylight's golden breath,
Slowly goes away—
Love of life, the light of love
Slowly drains away.
Night gives birth to peaceful death;
Night deposes day.

. . . . .

The clavicle of Solomon
Is open on my desk;
The head of John the Baptist
Has found its final rest.

. . . . .

A pentacle of Jupiter
Is cast upon the earth
And thereon lays Adoniel
To represent its worth.

. . . . .

A catacomb of misery
Inhabits all my head;
It represents a mystery
Of love in Psyche's stead.

. . . . .

At times the heart's despotic and overrules the brain.
"Love's like a narcotic"—admittance of a pain
That languishes beneath love's narcotizing spell,
A tacit affirmation that loveless life is hell.

. . . . .

A pentagram of blackened blood
Is scorched upon my heart
(An elemental darkened mood
Of which I am a part)
Transmuted into starry night
That vanishes in flame
In manner strange and recondite
And never seen again.

NOCTURNE No. 9

NOCTURNE No. 9

Summer is something to suffer through
From May until September;
Suffering summer is what you do
Until comes grey November.

Something is suffering in the gloom
That none dare to remember,
Suffering something to bring to bloom
What winter will dismember—

Suffer the summer to bring to bloom
What winter will dismember;
Suffer the summer until its tomb
Is buried in December.

The light lays waste to all our joys,
Reducing them to ember;
Retain in night what day destroys
Lest it's reduced to cinder.

Night and winter bring delight
That daylight cannot temper—
So give me frost and give me night—
Give me dark December.

Give me what the day destroys,
Give me dark December.
Summer's season just annoys;
It's winter I remember.

Suffering summer is what you do
Until comes grey November.
Summer is something to suffer through
From May until September.

"The grave shall not divide
us from
Life's sweetest pleasures, nor
has
It shielded us from loss'
bitterest tears.
We are connected through the
centuries,
And blood flows like years."

—from "The Vampiress," p. 189

NOCTURNE No. 10

NOCTURNE No. 10

Malkuth and Tiphereth

Stately Night's bridal gown flows deepest black
As she joins in her Satanic marriage.
The bridesmaids all whisper behind her back:
"A pale horse will drive for her carriage."

Demonic groomsmen gather like shadows
To join in the Satanic marriage.
Night's sister, Death, goes where Night goes;
A pale horse will drive for her carriage.

The band strikes a tune, celebrating a love
That the Devil could never disparage
(While beneath a bright moon in a black sky above
A pale horse arrives with their carriage).

But who is Night's groom? Time never tells—
Like an abattoir hid from its lairage.
A phantom of doom from the lowest of Hells?
The couple depart after marriage.

Stately Night's bridal train trails from her back
As she leaves in her honeymoon carriage.
Her raiments spill stars, her tear-stains are black
And she lovelessly succumbs to marriage.

NOCTURNE No. 11

"And black becomes the nighttime sky"

NOCTURNE No. 11

The Blue Hour and the Mortuarium of Night

When the blue hour arrives in cyanotype hues,
In drowsy shades, in watery blues
The earth sets to rest in civil twilight.

The mesosphere becomes a great skylight
And drowns all beneath in cælus' sapphire;
The Belt of Venus presents in sacrosanct fire
Around the horizon, ringed in blood red
Ere comes the night, dark as the dead.

And black becomes the nighttime sky
Like darkest imperial porphyry:
Obsidian and chalcedony,
Jet stone, onyx, ebony.
Daylight absconds, as if in ignominy,
A victim of twilight's sorcery.

NOCTURNE No. 12

"Twilight replaces the world we once knew."

NOCTURNE No. 12

Night — A Sonnet

Skies turn black; hedgerows grow grey; shadows fall;
    Objects disintegrate, fading from view.
Visions arise of a world 'neath a pall;
    Twilight replaces the world we once knew.
The earth turns its face away from the sun.
    Across the sky the moon shines but dimly.
Daylight showed life once, but now there is none—
    Neither daylight nor life, but nighttime grimly.

Silence blooms, gath'ring all in its calyx—
    Shadows fall; hedgerows grow grey; skies turn black—
Ere Chaos was Nothing, Night's pure radix[1]
    Might be seen could we but turn the clock back.
      And all would behold, at last, in their sight,
      A portrait of Death as perfect as Night.

---

[1] "Out of Chaos came Darkness and black Night, and out of Night came Light and Day, her children conceived after union in love with Darkness." — Hesiod, *Theogony*, 700 BCE

[2] Psalm 137:9 - New Living Translation of the Holy Bible.

NOCTURNE No. 13

"Dark and cruel, the devil's art — darker still, the human heart."

NOCTURNE No. 13

> And so of larger - Darknesses -
> Those Evenings of the Brain
> —DICKINSON

Darkness comes—the day does depart—
But darker still, the human heart.

Dark are night's spaces,
Which we've peopled aptly:
Vampires, werewolves, witches, and ghouls.
In lightless places
The credulous raptly
Listen to fairy tales, trembling as fools.

So darkness deludes us; we've all played a part.
But darkest of all is the human heart.

Shadows of nation-state, shadows of blood—
Projections of fancy and causes of war.
Blaming the devil and his evil brood
Exonerates him who's the war-machine's whore.

Darkness finds power when daytime departs,
But darker environs are in human hearts.

Evil may be afoot on the earth—
And who is not guilty? Who stands apart?
Satan is blamed, for what it is worth;
Yet darkest of devils is the human heart.

Dark and cruel, the devil's art—
Darker still, the human heart.

END

"And all would behold, at last,
in their sight
A portrait of Death as perfect
as Night."

—from "Nocturne No. 12," page 85

Notes for Thirteen Nocturnes:

The starres of the night
        Will lend thee their light,
    Like tapers cleare without number.
        —Robert Herrick, "The Night-Piece" (1648)

Wide are the meadows of night
        —Walter De La Mare, "The Wanderers" (ca. 1922)

Dead of midnight is the noon of thought.
        —Anna Laetitia Barbauld, "A Summer Evening's
            Meditation" (1773)

    The Bat that flits at close of Eve
    Has left the Brain that won't believe
    The Owl that calls upon the Night
    Speaks the Unbeliever's fright
        . . . . .
    Some are Born to sweet delight
    Some are Born to Endless Night
        —William Blake, "Auguries of Innocence" (1803)

    Once upon a midnight dreary
        —Edgar Allan Poe, "The Raven" (1845)

    Where an Eidolon, named NIGHT,
    On a black throne reigns upright
        —Edgar Allan Poe, "Dream-Land" (1844)

Notes for Thirteen Nocturnes (continued):

Come gentle death
In dead of night
And steal away
The morning light.
> —Rudimentary Peni, "No More Pain" (2008)

I bid the night conceive the glittering hemisphere.
> —Eliphas Levi, "The Magician" (ca. 1860s)

...night without end.
No dawn comes, night without end.
> —World Burns to Death, "Night Without End" (2003)

...The fresh warm blood in bowls, Aeneas sacrificed
A black-fleeced lamb to Night, the mother of the Furies,
And her great sister, Earth...
> —Virgil, *Aeneid*, Book VI (19 BCE)

Were all stars to disappear or die,
I should learn to look at an empty sky
And feel its total dark sublime...
> —W.H. Auden, "The More Loving One" (1957)

I sung of Chaos and Eternal Night,
Taught by the heav'nly Muse to venture down
The dark descent...
> — John Milton, *Paradise Lost* (1667)

The Void Cantos

"The nighttime sky reveals a black abyss—a threnody of black chalcedony"

THE DEAD STAR WHEEL

Now I want to sing of how I traveled beyond the sunset.

Some nights it rains red, very red, in my heart,
Red as a bright form of fire.

Some nights there is a blackness above that seems a mirror of all that's
black below.

Some nights I want to sing:

    The nighttime sky
      reveals a black abyss—
    A threnody
      of black chalcedony,
    A threnody
      of black chalcedony,
    A reverie
      of what is dead in me.

The stars are dying.
Time slows down.

The speed of light in
  a perfect vacuum decreases by
    half.

the nightmare sky

the red-form fire
that lies behind the horizon

I look at the sun below and it welters and is inflamed
Like an angry red rose.
The dark and ancient sun.

Its photosphere no longer seems a frightening or mysterious thing.

If you want to chase the sun you travel west.
If you want to greet the sun you travel east.
If you want to go beyond the sun—what then?

I brook no anger with fate.

I go faster than light and the starwheel dies around me. Its frozen corpse
glistens like a complicated diamond.

Out of the nightblack void of frozen stars and the
Still greater frozen empty spaces whose shining
        blackness
Weighs upon the cold blue haloed face of the earth—

Toward an area near Arcturus, where some stars hang
Off outside the Boötes Void like bundles
Of firethorn berries while others glimmer
The color of blue faience, trembling as if about
To fall apart or spill upon the earth in bundles
Of clear gemstones—a wellspring of glass shards—
Truest nighttime crawls forth,
A great and starry ghoul.

People have painted their faces white in the late Holocene epoch.

There is music, coarse as sandpaper,
        in the screeching of the celestial spheres
        and it comes to a stop,
        as broken as
        words commonly spoken.

I brook no hesitation with fate.

It rains red, very red, in my heart,
Red as a bright form of fire,
Bright as fire's reddest form.

REPRISAL

And then the sun came up in haste, like a reprisal
for what had happened
a few hours before, in the realm
Of black-shadow trees and impulses,
Vestigial, outmoded, from earlier in man's
Evolution, like the craving
For gluttonous amounts of
Sugar, fat, calories, salt,
Destruction, murder, war—bloodshed
Or deities, or our permanent teeth
That have to last 70 or more years but
Whose original design was meant
To last until maybe our 40s,
Holdovers that haunt our bodies,
And they all cause pain or disease in the end:
Phantom limbs lingering in our souls—instincts to murder, war, rape,
 territory, hatred; dominance.

Where have the moments gone?
(Starlight retreating, descending.)
Where are the years wasted to?
(Sunlight presenting, ascendant.)

There are stars as fiery as warfare
And anti-stars blacker than death, swirling out
Far from the earth's exurban sprawl, a
Self-important mistress of ceremonies absent from her
Own larger gala, locked in an infinite holocaust
But also weathering lonely aeons,
Where the infamous gallows of Tyburn
And the gibbet of Montfaucon
Are little red footnotes, little black
Helicoid tunnels to competing secret
Histories, locked in a struggle that
Never ends, O black eyes, O
Solemn sorcery, O well of gravity, O cryptic lifetimes.

NIHIL NEGATIVUM

> *Inter fæces et urinas nascimur.*
> ("We are born between feces and urine.")
>   —attributed to St. Augustine

Man and his generations,
     A caravansary of blood
   And flesh,
        Unending,
   Confronted at
Every turn by
          A melancholy void—
        Overcome, confused,
     Loathing himself to
Warfare, to suicide, and
                    giving himself up to
        Other necrolatry—

Man and his thoughts,
                His ideas deracinated—
                De-ratiocinated—at
                Every angle by
                    a melancholy void.

The uttermost darkness of space presses its face close to the
            earth, its history in full view of the septillion
        glistering
     stars
        that
          he did not make, could not make,
                but which he must watch helplessly at night from afar.

Man and man's issue,
An utter No-thing.

CANTO OF 99942-APOPHIS
An Orison

(In 2004, scientists predicted that on Friday the 13th, 2029, an asteroid named 2004-MN4 had a decent chance of striking the earth, possibly triggering a global extinction event, depending on the location of impact. The asteroid was renamed 99942-Apophis. Since 2004 scientists have publicly said that revised calculations have reduced the chance of its impact to zero.)

> Humanity's self-alienation has reached such a degree that it can
> experience its own destruction as an aesthetic pleasure of the
> first order.
> —WALTER BENJAMIN, "The Work of Art
> in the Age of Mechanical
> Reproduction" (1936)

99942-Apophis—*destroy us.*

Put an end to our *Disseminated Primatemaia*,
To *homo rapiens*,
To the pestilence of hominids
And hominids' concomitant malice.

99942-Apophis—*wreck us.*
Destroy our animal illusions,
Our bacterial and viral selves,
The endless misery of life,
Of our lives,
The unreasonable mysteries of life
That haunt us and harry us—
Let our worries and uncertainty cease.

Smash us.
Let there be
A quiet darkness in
    this universe of flame, frost, and pain,
    this universe of life gathered up against

the towering shadow of decay,
of life always wilting in death's
constant company.

Let there be
cold silence
and the nostrum of cold silence,
the absolute silence of space
and its endless blackness
in place of the earth,

the cruelless cold of
existence without man
or the terror of his reality,
a reality that is a terror to him,
and a reality that is made a terror by him—

the terror of his own
brain against himself, his own
meat rotting around him, his own ideas
causing misfortune for himself
and others, of his
own wars despoiling, his own
bloody-mindedness, his own
dark plans persistently brooding,

of diseases assailing him and
diseases of his own making besetting him,
of his own sanity deserting him
to make his mind a kind of ghoul-haunted waste.

99942-Apophis—*destroy us.*
99942-Apophis—*wreck us.*
99942-Apophis—*smash us.*

In the nightmare of your strong form descending,
In the portent of your black form circling,
In the augury of your horror approaching,
Let us glimpse the final grace,

And let us become pure nothing in your vastation.
99942-Apophis—*smash us.*

I obtest to you,
99942-Apophis, charnel serpent,
Apep, uncreator in primal darkness,
Aten-class asteroid or ancient Dragon of Chaos,
Let us labor no more for our
Own self-mutilation, as it were—for our own
Self-immolation, for our own self-annihilation,
Our callow *selbstmord,*
For our own childish efforts at understanding,
For our own childish pretensions to enlightenment—
For our own cloying delusions,
For our own childishness.

99942-Apophis, charnel serpent,
Apep, uncreator in primal darkness—
Come down from your perihelion,
Descend and sound the trumpet-call;
You can conclude our slow suicide unfolding.

Usher us into starry graves;
Make us dissolve back into the interstellar medium
From which we arose.
You can be our Wormwood Star,
Our thirteen-rayed star of death,
Our dark star falling;
And inaugurate the seventh and final, blessèd
Extinction event—make it as if the
Third angel had sounded his trumpet
To bring down the bitter star to
Change a third of the waters into bitterness—
Unseal the Seventh Seal, the last and greatest,
The coda to the Anthropocene Extinction,
In this, our Holocene Epoch—in this,
Our Holocaust Epoch.
Rain down death like snowfall,
Cause the sky to collapse upon us,

Make the Hechaloth implode in
Infinite burning rains
On this planet of hideous hatred, hell, harm—
In this existence of enmity, antipathy, apathy, and disgust,
In this life of disease, death, rapine, and war,
In this farce.
Raze the walls and the prisons we've built,
The strictures of class, and religion, and gender,
Of nation, race, and tribe—all the accidents of
Birth, of time and place, all the misfortunes of
Time and place, the bodies into
Which we've been placed adventitiously, the places and
Circumstances, the precarious economic straits,
With Death always lurking in the wings
When indigency is not—
The vicissitudes we endure or even the very era of history into
Which we are thrown (this strange *geworfenheit*)—*annihilate them.*
Annihilate this.
Incinerate the species. Obliterate our destiny.

You can set the horizon to fire;
You can inaugurate the post-hominid era.

99942-Apophis—*destroy us.*
99942-Apophis—*wreck us.*
99942-Apophis—*smash us.*

WAR UNIVERSE
A Cento

This is a war universe.
War all the time.
War was always here. Before man was, war waited for him.
> The ultimate trade awaiting its ultimate practitioner.
War is our scourge; yet war has made us wise.
Yesterday the Sabbath of witches; but to-day the struggle.

We are the dead; short days ago
On that poor world we scorn yet die to shield—
Singing. The Sun has left his blackness, & has found a
> fresher morning.
I am the enemy you killed, my friend.
What are days for?
Where is paradise? There is no paradise
I ask you: Do you want total war? If necessary, do you want
> war more total and radical than anything that we can
> even yet imagine?
Your darkness, which you did not suspect since it was dead,
> will come to life and you will feel the crush of total evil
Like other animals, we are embodiments of universal Will,
> the struggling, suffering energy that animates
> everything—
human beings: uniforms, boots.
One dies of war like any old disease.
Beat the wild war-drums made of serpent's skin.

[Sources: Line 1: William S. Burroughs, "The War Universe"; Line 2: Poison Idea— *War All the Time* LP; Line 3: Cormac McCarthy, *Blood Meridian, or the Evening Redness in the West*; Line 4: Sigfried Sassoon, "Absolution"; Line 5: W.H. Auden, "Spain"; Line 6: John McCrae, "In Flanders Fields"; Line 7: Alan Seeger, "On Returning to the Front After Leave"; Line 8: William Blake, "America"; Line 9: Wilfred Owen, "Strange Meeting"; Line 10: Philip Larkin, "Days"; Line 11: Joseph Goebbels, 1943 Sportpalast speech; Line 12: Ai Qing, "Faith"; Line 13: C.G. Jung, *Liber Primus*; Line 14: John Gray, *Straw Dogs*; Line 15: Dan Pagis, "Testimony"; Line 16: Wilfred Owen, "A Terre"; Line 17: Henry Wadsworth Longfellow, "The Arsenal at Springfield"]

NOVEMBER SONG

November was the season, separate all its own,
With soft gray rains
That came before snow
And washed our Autumn from the year.

November's somber reason, as we have come to know,
Involves the strains
Of lovers' woes
And mourning after tears.

CANTO OF ASMODEUS
(or, New Proverbs of Hell)

In The Marriage of Heaven and Hell, *William Blake wrote, "As I was walking among the fires of Hell ... I collected some of their Proverbs; thinking that as the sayings used in a nation mark its character, so the Proverbs of Hell show the nature of Infernal wisdom better than any description of buildings or garments." My own encounter with Asmodeus one night—in a quiet grove ringed by dead, leafless, and gnarled live oak trees in East Texas—yielded these further Proverbs from the Infernal Country.*

In far East Texas there's
A town called Elysian Fields, so-named
By a Captain from New Orleans who,
In the 1830s, found the spot to be a
Perfect idyll. Once, I traveled there en route
To Louisiana and stopped by a
Trailer Park to rest. Just outside the edge
Of the Trailer Park two dead Live-Oaks
Formed a sort of massive pair of Horns,
Noticeable from the Highway.
In the crook of the two horn-like Trees,
There sat Asmodeus, whittling—
Whistling, whittling, and waiting.
 'There are Proverbs and Psalms of
Hell for people such as yourself,' he said
While turning to me. 'Which do you
Want?' 'Proverbs,' I answered.
'*Praesignis!* The Psalms will come later.'

I.

Individuality is a blessing. It spares you from knowing the thoughts of
Others.

Blessed are the Deaf: They cannot hear Others' lies. Blessed are the Mute—they cannot speak them.

Praise the Coffin-Worm for its appetite. Excoriate the Flower for its pride.

Terrible are the actions of Men. But worse are Men's thoughts.

Be not proud of who you are. Is the Pupa proud of itself? No—it wants to become a Butterfly!

The desire for Vengeance—a healthy regard for the Self.

Propriety denies. Evil allows.

The scheming of Others will be revealed to All in time.

II.

The gardens of Orthodoxy are fragrant with hypocrisy. The groves of Heterodoxy are sumptuous with truth.

Sunlight burns. Moonlight heals.

Let him who tolls the Bell be first to respond to its ringing.

Emptiness of Soul is not a curse; the Soul is a Chimæra.

War is the State of Nature. Peace is the State of Exception.

Take heed: Be wary of those easily roused to Anger by things they do not understand.

The Home represents Danger. The Fortress represents Strength. The Dragon represents Friendship.

Could Humanity but look into its collective heart, War would never cease.

The Moon is a grateful planet—grateful that nothing lives on it!

III.

Let him who organizes the race, run it. Let him who prepares the meal, devour it. Let him who finds the lost article, keep it.

Most of that which is human is Ugliness, and is Undesirable.

Poverty is a gift to man; it teaches Innovation. But lucky are those born in the shadow of Death, the most sublime Teacher!

As the tree lets go of its heaviest fruit, so should one let go of their heaviest burdens.

The greater the Mask, the greater the Person.

Destruction: Without it, there is nothing. And with only Destruction, there is also nothing.

The Sun would be just as content without the Earth buzzing about it.

The Self is a fortress assailed by all Else.

As drowsiness is to Sleep, so Peace is to War.

IV.

The Blind Man seeks Wisdom in Images; the Deaf Man seeks Wisdom in Music. The Wise Man seeks wisdom in No-thing.

To the unenlightened, power comes from strength. But the wise know true strength comes from deception.

They say that youth is wasted on the young. Ah, but death is wasted on the dead!

Happy is he who takes your babies and smashes them against the rocks![2]

The tree is not resentful of the birds that take its fruits. Be like the tree!

The shadow of Life is Death; and Death evinces its jealousy of Life through the phenomenon of Disease.

Earth circles a Brightness. But that Brightness circles a Darkness, and that Darkness spins along the gyre of a Greater Darkness outside it.

"THE REST OF MY YEARS..."

The rest of my years
For a grove or some place,
A grove ringed with cypresses
Tall, gaunt, and grim—
Or some place more quiet
Even than this.
A place where the trees
Hold sadness at bay,
And death's gladsome day
Departs with the breeze.

CANTO OF BELPHEGOR

The child descends
From the woman
In robes of blood.

CANTO OF BELIAL

The man descends
From the ape
In rivers of blood.

"This is a death universe."

DEATH UNIVERSE

This is a death universe.
Death all the time.
Death was always here. Before man was, death waited for
    him. The ultimate station awaiting its ultimate
    voyager.
Death is our scourge; yet death has made us wise.
Yesterday the Sabbath at church; but to-day the funeral.

We are the foolish; short days ago
On that war-ravaged world we scorn yet die to shield—
Weeping. The Moon has left her blackness, & has found a
    fresher midnight.
I am the friend you killed, my enemy.
What are nights for?
Where is hell? There is no hell
I ask you: Do you want total death? If necessary, do you want
    death more total and radical than anything that we can
    even yet imagine?
Your darkness, which you did not suspect since it was dead, will
    come to life and you will feel the crush of total death.
Like other animals, we are embodiments of universal death, the
    struggling, suffering enervation that animates
    everything—
human beings: uniforms, boots.
Death.
Play the funeral march on flutes of hollowed bone.

[Note: See "War Universe: A Cento" on page 109.]

"a cathedral despair—a church of the nonexistence"

ABYSS

a black delirium,
madness—starlight and madness.
madness that manifests under starlight.

blasts of cold rain—
lancets of blood—
blood and cold rain, battering
windows—beating in
my head—

a pounding as of hundreds of hammers
on sheet metal, or iron—like metal pounded for
panzers, for siege machines—
a rain of blows—
blood and rain and fire—
a fire against the unwholesome sky—
death unwholesome—death fulsomely—
fulsomely manifest—
through pain—through purity—
through pain's purity

pain, despair, and drunkenness—
a black self-destruction—
anger and impotent fury—and
circles of anger like malebolge
wrapped oppressively round my head—

death resplendent—
death triumphant—or death everlasting—
destruction and blackness—
blackness refulgent—the scintillating blackness

"a church of death—the worship of death—prayers to death and its blackness"

of deepening despair—
a cathedral despair—a church of the nonexistence—

a church of death—the worship of death—
prayers to death and
its blackness—
its beauty and efflorescence, its
essence, its
brute darkness, its florid bruteness

tombstones preoccupy me—where
does their darkness lead?—their austerity,
their severity—
the severity and the austerity
of tombs, their final darkness,
their brazen display

a delirium of the spiraling abyss—the
helix, the blood-red helix—rain,
bloody rain—the impression of
madness—

sensual madness—
have you felt the impression
of madness on your brain? — there
is an abyss that churns the very-ness—
space, matter—it violently devours

blood and fire
with silver—
blood-fire, silver fire, the abyss—

blackness, ultimate bloody blackness—
blood-red blackness, blue-red like the high
onyx of her nails polished—and blue-black—
an abyss of black flame—
chaos, torture, starlight

the stars are impure—sin and myself.

"In my twenties, I lost my mind to madness"

VOID CANTO

In my twenties, I lost my mind to madness.
(But—I played sly tricks on madness.[3])

Blood haunted my thoughts, and
Anger distorted my reason.
Images of murder, bloody cruelty, and
Extremities of all kinds plagued
My dreams. I grew weary with life.

My twenties were like a
Dark forest that was untended
And had grown choked with
Brush, with nocuous plants,
Brambles, and thorns that
Closed off all avenues
Of egress.

I came to a dark tarn in
The center of the wood.
Thirsty, I drank its black
And cold water.

Where could the very sigils I had
Traced onto my skin have come from,
If not transmitted to me
In red, in deathly dreams from Caina, from
Avernus' lowest depths?

Have you not seen
That above the sky
There is another sky,

---

[3] "I played sly tricks on madness." —Rimbaud, "A Season in Hell" (1873) (Louise Varèse trans.)

A second sky—
A black sky, infinite in its darkness?

I drank the cold waters
Of the black tarn in the forest
Of midnight. My flesh shivered.

When I cut myself open
The black waters poured from
Me; but they had become red.

My body, it seems, was the supreme alchemist;
Or perhaps I was like Christ,
But in reverse—an Anti-christ:
Water had changed to blood
Inside my body, which I spilled
Back into the soil.

"Have you not seen
That above the sky
There is another sky,
A second sky—
A black sky, infinite
in its darkness?"

—from "Void Canto," page 125

CANTO OF ASTAROTH

> To me life is evil.
>> —GIACOMO LEOPARDI, "Night-Song of A Wandering
>> Shepherd of Asia" (1830)

The four beasts that
Stood about the
Throne of the Lamb during
The Eschaton, and who each,
In their turn, announced, *Come and see!*
Grew agèd. They eventually died.

From their four rotting carcasses black
Ichors trickled, and the four winds
Of Heaven and Earth ceased.
The four cardinal directions
Collapsed upon themselves.
A black cataract revealed a charnel infinity.

But one direction did remain—
Toward the starless void of Astaroth.

THE DEAD STAR AROUND WHICH WE ALL REVOLVE

For Sagittarius A*

There's a dead star up
In the sky above—
    It's true, it's true—
A dead star whose power is greater than love,
        up in the sky above.

There's a dead star around
Which we all revolve—
    Yes, it's true—
A dead star whose riddles admit no resolve,
        up in the sky above.

There's a black star out
Deep in space whose call—
    Yes, it's true—
Is answered by Sol and its eight planets, all
        up in our sky above.

There's a dark, dreaming mass
At our galaxy's center—
    Yes, it's true—
A place where light dies once it has entered—
        up in our sky above—

A central darkness glowing,
With blackened rays outgoing
Like Hades' rivers flowing,
And vacua all showing...

...A darkness that draws
Outer light to its core—
    Yes, it's true—

To death in its coffin forevermore,

> devouring all starlight,
> holding fast to twilight
> sprawling wide in midnight,
> up in the sky above.

CANTO OF 333-CHORONZON

Roiling fires pour'd into the Void,
Ancient and infinite, from all directions,
Their shapes intangible, liquid,
Sloughing off an immense form of heat,
Flames as phantoms of light and shadow,
Revealing nothing of the
Greater nullity of the fixed stars, of
The greater nihility of earth and its wars.
The fires of the Abyss are
Not like the flames of Earth:
Earthly flames are incandescent;
And they emit Light. The flames
Of the Abyss are black; and
They radiate Shadow.

I sought for myself a share
Of the undimensioned Black Flame,
That I might draw its blackness inside my Mind.
(Black is the bloodiness of flame/
Bloody is the eternal flame's blackness.)

The black flame on my tongue,
I rejoiced: O blue eyes of my love,
O blue love of my eyes, I swallow
You. And it did burn a blackness
Through me, growing into
A consuming Void that
Roiling fires pour'd into.

My flesh split open: I began to shine
Like a Wolf-Rayet star, like an
Exposed helium core aflame under
Intense radiation pressure. I thought
I saw a century of blood-webbed wings
Lifting things aloft into the second
And third skies outside what is visible
To domesticated eyes.

"The space of my heart was dark and starry"

CANTO OF SAMAEL

It was in a time when
I had sought for solitude
Among the living, and among
What was commonplace.

I was intoxicated with
The ocean, and I saw that
There was an ocean inside me, too.
But my spirit wilted like
A rose uncared for.

There was mercy in my peregrinations:
I found my desires
Had turned from
Outer objects towards those
Things that are within me.
The space of my heart
Was dark and starry
As a midnight sky,
But it was a sky in the
Middle of a violent transformation.

The stars winked out
And there was a great black space,
A vestigial void where
Once my life's blood pumped.
There was an ocean of absence
There, great and black.

In that ocean's depths I
Found Samael, arch-demon of
The lower altitudes,
Sleeping as if in hibernation. His
Crown of human
Bone, of desiccated lilies

Had slipped from his brow.

When I saw him, I
Knew I had reached
The very place

      of the
        Soul.
Samael awoke.

          And
          What

          He said to
          to Me—

          what he w h i s p e r e d—
          to *me*—

              was *madness*

                ..

*Sgr A**

sgr a*:

the schwarzschild radius of sagittarius a*—

$$R_S = \frac{2G <}{c^2}$$

and the entropy of its dead, dark form—

$$S = \frac{kc^3 A}{4Gh}$$

sgr a*'s temperature—:

$$T = \frac{hc^3}{8\pi kGM}$$

CXOGC J174536.1-285638
viewing its nothingness
from earth:
right ascension: $17^h\ 45^m\ 12^s$
declination: $-28°\ 48'\ 18''$

look up! there's a hole in the sky,
and it swings us around
its light that is not.

NIGHT-PIECE BENEATH STARLIGHT (2018)

> Putrefaction is the end
> Of all that nature doth intend.
> —ROBERT HERRICK, "Putrefaction" (1648)

I could have built a cemetery
With all the memories I've buried.

O wasn't there a time
When things weren't this way—
When things weren't so desolate,
So desperate?
Some nights it rains black, very black,
In my heart,
Black as a dark form of fire,
Black as fire's darkest form.[4]
You could lower my heart into Hades,
Or put on my corpse a crown
Of poplar twigs, dead lilies—
And imagine a funeral dirge
Composed solely of snowfall
And hemlock—or only of cold rain, or
The ghosts of imaginary summers.

O, the time has passed—and wasn't there once a time?

I could have bled black forever
When I read your letter
About our last days together.

---

[4] See the closing lines of "The Dead Starwheel" on page 100.

I could have built great tombs
To stand beneath thousands of moons.

My emotions swell, subside, play havoc,
Like an ignis fatuus—like
Shadows that clamor at dusk
For the nighttime, for their own time;
But which canter away,
Too, at the dawn before sunlight.
You could lower my body into the earth
And pour on my grave
A libation bitter—
A sour pour condign
Of absinthe and Malbec wine—
Mixed together and become sour as this heart of mine,
Absinthe and Malbec wine.

O, the time has passed—
And haven't there been better times?

...Wasn't there once a time...?

I could have bled black forever
When I read your letter
About our final days together.
I could have made a cemetery
Out of all of these memories now buried.

I could have built great tombs
To stand beneath infinite moons.

"THERE IS A THING DECEASED THAT I DREAM OF…"

For Georg Trakl

There is a thing deceased that I dream of
A mountain lies far away
A red candle burns in the window
The live-oaks stand gaunt and dead

Wind chimes sound softly at evening;
It's 10:30 at night, says the clock
My cat lies asleep on the footrest
A shadow floats down the hallway

Crowding my mind—there are memories
—the moon boasts an icy glow—
Of a thing deceased, in my dreams—
And grey leaves patter on windows

In my yard, a snow-capped headstone
The stars seem brittle and frozen
The house has a draft, I believe (I should fix this)
A mirror sits over the fireplace

The mirror's empty blackness
Reflects the red candle, alone

AFTER THE SPECIES

> Species cannot control their fates. Species do not exist.
> —JOHN GRAY, *Straw Dogs* (2003)

I am
  As now,
    Ever.

    Ever,
Or never.

      (Ever
      Now,
        Am I.)

Never
 (Is) now,
 Or ever.

Never—ever—forever.

"The shirred meat of history fell upon the valley floor"

CANTO OF GEHENNA
A Canto in Four Parts

I. *Beneath Gehenna's Sepulchering Sky*

Beneath Gehenna's sepulchering sky
The pyrolatrous Kings of Judah gave
Their children over to sacrifice and fire. A
Dark black star shone above all; and in
The black star's thrall the shadows
Themselves produced shadows.
From the bladebones of the slaughtered children,
Which were blanched ghostly white by a
Hot sun now expired, their skeletal remains
Littered upon the burntblack scoria
Of the valley floor but also climbing
High onto the surrounding hillsides where
They glinted out like night-scented orchids,
The dead children of the Kings of Judah
Recalled the before-times, when they did not
Know of the procession of expiration
From the high azimuth of life to its
Bloody caesura at the end
At the hands of their fathers.
Existence lies elsewhere, they sang:
Never—ever—forever.

II. *Beneath Gehenna's Sky, Grey As Mortuary Wax*

Beneath Gehenna's sky grey as adipocere,
Grey as ash, as filthy-grey as kerogen or
Other organic material long decomposed—
Grey as oil swirled with human cremains—
Genocide and Homicide, twin numina,

Came upon the land.

The shirred meat of history fell upon
The valley floor.
Existence lies elsewhere, a dead soldier sang:
Never—ever—forever.

Homicide, bearing a flared scarlet pennon,
Spoke of the fresh bleeding of
Murdered bodies in the presence of
Their killers, of the cruentation of corpses.
Thus spake Homicide—of death's
Long journey to earth, and how the
Earth provided a pleasant caravansary
For its stay, and ample blood for its refection.
"The stars rifle near to the Earth like
The torches of a search party gathering towards
The discovery of a body"—
Thus spaketh Homicide.

Thus spaketh Genocide: "The stars gather
Close to the earth like torches
Traveling toward a Black Mass."
The black mass at the galactic center
Extended a ghostly Orion-arm
To draw the earth to its breast.

Genocide's deep black gonfalon was
Hemmed by swastikas incarnadine;
And, on closer inspection, the ancient
Vedic symbols revealed themselves transformed
Into the eternal Flag of the Nation-State.
Genocide's voice was black as melena:
"Blood is not dark enough for my design.
War is the health of the Race. War is the
Health of the Tribe. War is the health of
Property. War is the health of Territoriality.
War is the health of personhood. War is health,
Corporate. War is the health of life. War is the

Health and the hell; war is the hell and the health."

The machinery of Heaven and Hell began
To click and whir; all things were
Set into motion. Dark engineers constructed
A complex scaffolding of burnt bone around the
Large-scale structure of the cosmos. The
First quantum object winked like
A bloody star *in utero*.

Thus spaketh Homicide: "The sun rises east
Of Eden and sets west of Europe. The winter
Wind, the cries of slaughter, withered lips,
The spent biology of the human organism,
The zoology of nuclear destruction, the
Nuclear zoology of DNA and decomposition"—
His words were scattered like pebbles,
Like point-particles bouncing across a broad spectrum.

III. *Man made his gods*

"Man made his gods," Xenophanes
Wrote in Greece in the 5th century BCE.
And this is true: People make their gods.
There are gods inside of people,
Demons inside of people, spermatozoa, eggs,
Blood, brain tissue, bone that can be
Pounded to powder or burnt to ash, or bones
That can be sharpened to weapons
Once the muscle has been stripped from them;
And flesh that can melt or decompose or be
Cooked and devoured by others to provide
Calories, energy, life.

IV. *Erebus*

EREBUS. The moon from the night sky would I sever,
That light might not shine forth there, ever.
Obliterate starlight from the æther.
Night should be darkness, pure and forever. [5]

---

[5] THAUMIEL. You are the universe moving
In love and in infinite night;
You are a human living
In a time of hideous hate.
You are a beacon shining;
You are a season changing;
You are a new moon rising;
You are winter dreaming;
You are a vast horizon;
You are a complex prison;
You are a petrel gliding;
You are a lodestar winking;
You are a new way forming;
You are a poison coursing;
You are a graveyard yawning;
You are a sunrise glowing;
You are the universe moving
In love and in infinite night;
You are a human being
In a hideous time of hate.

ISRAFEL. *You may not obtain all that you desire,*
But you can set the horizon to fire;
And if there are flames left over from this,
You can construct a fiery abyss.
And if there are flames left over from that,
Gird thyself for the Amduat.

NOCTURNE No. 14

> Here in the night are the seven wonders of the world
> —ROBERT DESNOS, "The Spaces Inside Sleep" (1926)

the colors of battered flesh
swell in the heavens.
the sky goes from blue to black
throughout the course of a day,
a canopy of bruises:
battered flesh and starlight,
as if bruising becomes midnight.

the sunset in summer—a gunshot wound of color,
like a burst blood vessel.
later the sky weeps salty rain,
grieving, after it greys like
the hair of someone that's witnessed
murder. (which it has—108 billion times.)
violence can be associated with astronomical
phenomena in other
ways; when one is hit especially hard
they're said to see stars. some
bruises are yellow, green,
and brown, and sometimes the sky is grey.
(bruises can also be grey.)
stars can also shine yellow and green;
and there are brown dwarf stars, as well.

battered flesh and starlight,
as if bruising becomes midnight
or the blackness of necrotic flesh, when
the sun disappears and night marshals
darkness to itself, when flags and eyes
are lowered, when to actually look up
at midnight is like peering into the
crematory's final black retort.

"The Cross of Blood, the Cross of Shadow has oft made war, and oft made widow"

THE CROSS OF BLOOD

The Cross of Blood,
The Cross of Shadow
Has oft made war,
And oft made widow.
Iron cross
Or hakenkreuz
First deceives,
Then destroys;
For some the flag
Acts as a cross,
And in its name
A holocaust.

"Fruit of a nightmare"

RULES FOR THE HUMAN ZOO
A Canto of Warfare Comprised of Five Haiku

> At the heart of humanism we discover a cult or club of fantasy.
> —PETER SLOTERDIJK, "Rules for the Human Zoo" (2001)

> The absolute freedom of the human creature is horrible.
> —ALEJANDRA PIZARNIK, "The Bloody Countess" (1971)

Fragment of a Scene from the Kursk Salient, 1943

Vehicular death
Tangled limbs, metal, blood-smeared.
Odor: Burnt black oil.

PzKpfw II

Black Maybach engine
Creaking, gears grinding,
Fire-breathing demon.

The Lost Armies of Europe

The lost armies of
Europe march on silent plains,
Night Victorious.

Jagdpanther

Severe grey angles
Turretless malevolence
Squat steel gunned bulwark

Victory in Smolensk

Fruit of a nightmare:
Blackened machinery strewn
Like junkyard leavings.

THE CENTRAL PARSEC

Hence in the smallest circle, where the point is
Of the Universe, upon which Dis is seated...
—DANTE

The murderer fell to his knees
And implored forgiveness from the cross.
The cross itself was positioned on the
Church wall several feet off the ground
At the back of the chancel.
The simple, unadorned Latin cross
Was plain, but heavy; and
The murderer fell before it in regret.
The cross remained stoic and unanswering,
Mute to all entreaties offered.
Its presence was somehow
All the more severe because of this.
The murderer took the cross's silence
As an answer. His mourning spirit
Did not want to know the symbol was a
Vestige of an appeal to the supernatural,
Or a relic of a time now past. He
Did not know that the cross to which
He obtested was not a radio to a deity.
His eyes, like his murders, produced tears,
And in his misery he prostrated himself
Before the stark and impotent emblem.
25, 640 light years away, in
The galaxy's central parsec (in fact, at
The "density cusp of quiescent X-ray binaries
In the central parsec of the galaxy")
Sagittarius A*, the supermassive black hole
Turning at the Milky Way's center, weltered
Like a cancerous ulcer in the pit
Of a stomach, devouring the surrounding
Light, growing in its mysterious darkness,

Sending its close-hugged orbiting stars
Into a frenzied snarl of activity. In
The galaxy's Orion Arm, where earth's
Beloved and life-giving Sol makes
One revolution around that dark star
Every 233 million years, Karl Jansky
Turned his radio array to the galactic center
And heard the black hole's thick hissing.
It was like a plague of tinnitus, or like a
Serpent warning an approaching human
Of its presence.

AN INFINITE RADIUS

> Dark is life, dark, dark is death.
> —JOHN HAWKES, *The Cannibal* (1949)

> Floating round the Universe
> Fucking in our Cosmic Hearse
> —RUDIMENTARY PENI, *"Cosmic Hearse"* (1983)

NOR ARE THERE to be any halcyon
times ahead, my friend:

    the arc of an infinite radius————

                —is a straight line

    in a future; removed far

                —this, not the future, the—

      aeon: the new aeon, the red aeon
        now, the anthropocene;
        comes the anthropocene extinction, (and, with it,

part and parcel) the
      anthropocene extinctinction event

      mutant humans (mutation 1: language acquisition—
          the FOXP2 gene in Chromosome 7)

   that might still be hominids
   but the skies are orange in the far future, filtration sacs

(mutation 2) process
contaminated/filthy/polluted air

the winging of the scapula (pre-mutation 3)

—this, not the future, the—

pupula duplex (mutation 4)

the Final Man may be alive now;

time in eternal recurrence

the Russian cosmists should be happy: man can fly unaided in
hazardous orange skies

black form (I)
red form (II)
the scapula transforms into the wingbone (mutation

3)

blood—and rain—and fire terrible:

In the infinite planar face
Of an infinite holy space—
The circumference of an infinite sphere,
A hypersphere grown clear
Of limiting hemispheres—

The arrow of time moves[6]
Along on the path of
An infinite radius;
And the radius of an infinite or eternal circle
Is a straight line

---

[6] "Let us draw an arrow arbitrarily. If, as we follow the arrow, we find more and more of the random element in the state of the world, then the arrow is pointing towards the future; if the random element decreases the arrow points towards the past. That is the only distinction known to physics. This follows at once if our fundamental contention is admitted that the introduction of randomness is the only thing which cannot be undone. I shall use the phrase 'time's arrow' to express this one-way property of time which has no analogue in space." — Arthur Eddington, *The Nature of the Physical World* (1928)

(the point at infinity is death,
O light of the final way!
watch the circline close upon itself at
cosmic death, an Ouroboros serpent,
O light of
the highest way!)

The circumference of an infinite sphere,
A hypersphere—a sphere
Of extra- (or ultimate) dimensions
Assumes, too, the form of
An infinite radius;
And it constitutes time's arrow, a
Straight line traveling through.[7]

Now for the resurrection of the dead[8]

Drinking alone in my bedroom: A corpse twists in space against a radiant vortex that, itself, churns slowly behind it. It's a vision that recurs nightly and I've progressed from a solid 13% ABV Cabernet Sauvignon to a much sturdier Malbec that pushes the limits of respectability at 19% alcohol. Sleep eludes me. (*Life* eludes me!) If this carries on, soon I will be drinking whiskey neat, and the silence in my bedroom will become so loud that I'll want to meet with a doctor to see if I have tinnitus. (But might the doctor

---

[7] Time is a terrible master;
  He speaks of an imminent end.
  Time urges, "Live your life faster,"
  But proves he's a miserly friend.

[8] My heart is a prostitute's garden—
  My conscience a dark forest's warden;

  My face is a funeral mask;
  My love an apocalypse black.

respond, "You do not have tinnitus; you are hearing what Robert Jansky heard when he pointed his radio array toward the galactic center"? *O Sagittarius A*!*)

The corpse slowly tumbles, night after night, hanging in the darkness but rotating as if its winding sheets are being unspooled by phantom hands. The aerial ballet performed by the floating body gives the impression of something like a cross between a swan filmed in slow motion and medical waste tumbling down to the bottom of the ocean, bandages and bloody detritus streaming slowly in the water behind it. I'm not sure whose corpse it is; in the dreams I say to myself, "We're not advanced enough to be this far out in space. I must be dreaming of the future."

The luminous void behind the suspended corpse rotates, too. (And that is so much of what existence is—objects rotating, circling, revolving, pirouetting, spiraling, all along their appointed gyres. The moon circles the earth; the earth circles the sun; the sun circles Sagittarius A*; Sagittarius A* probably circles something in the Laniakea Supercluster, which may revolve around something in the Great Attractor near Norma in the southern celestial hemisphere— *O Abell 3627!*)

One night the corpse speaks to me and says it will find me; that it will begin its journey to me through the vast gulfs of space along *the path of an infinite radius.* (*Non est ad terris mollis e astra via.*) I wake up in a cold sweat: I remember that the path of an infinite radius is a straight line. I resolve to drink Malbec and whiskey no more; I'll drink Lacrima di Morro d'Alba instead!

So, it seems I have avoided the fearful thing in dreams. But it does not want to be avoided any longer.

The daimon of my mind, known as Cruciel,
Cradled in fire as if
In boiling clouds of hydrogen,
Sings the following, sweetly, as if from a lectionary:

> This is your autumn, and you must suffer—
> To new gods forming you must find offer.

Soon comes your winter when you must proffer
Yourself to Death and declare this all over.

> ...And so Cruciel was extinguished;
> And a kind of death did sweep over me.

Abasdarhon assumed the place of Chrymos
In the black skies
And praised the dark waters
That flow like black liquors
Above Heaven, and which pour into
The heavens like rivers of blood.
And the demon-angel[9] Chrymos sang:

> Life is a night
> Blacker than black
> (Alas and alack.)

The demon Abbaton—who in Heaven
Had long ago been called Mouriel, and
Who now asserted a kingship over
Death itself; and whose "eyes and face
Are like revolving wheels of fire"[10] —

—the sun itself is a freezing fire entombed beneath the purple waters of
the ocean, drifting toward the eastern horizon—

Spoke:

---

[9] "'Demons,' 'angels'—these are just words we use for different entities." —Kenneth Anger, talk at UCLA, 2009

[10] "The exception was Mouriêl, to whom God Himself afterwards gave the name of 'Abbaton'... At that time Abbaton was a seven-headed monster, with projecting teeth and tusks nearly a foot long, with eyes and face like revolving wheels of fire, whose snortings were like the crackling of flames in a lake of boiling sulphur and bitumen, and whose breathings were like unto seven thunders. Whenever he appeared to men they died immediately of fright, for his hideousness, and cruelty, and mercilessness terrified everyone." —from the *Discourse on Abbaton* by Timothy, Archbishop of Alexandria, ca. 380 CE.

I have no loyalty to humans, angels, or any deities;
I am loyal only to gradations of suffering.
Who oils the hinges to the trapdoors to Hell?

Spoke:

Who oils the hinges to the trapdoors to Hell?
Who bolts shut the gates to Heaven?
Each noiseless opening of the trapdoors to Hell
Occurs in perfect silence;
Every denial of entry to Heaven: perfect silence.

Spoke:

You are human bacterium.[11]
There are special plans for an unskinned human;
There are designs kept in a hidden chamber in Hell;
Winged humans, and the dead resurrected.

> (Elsewhere, the teeth of Achlys chatter
>   In the black frozen waste; to her
>   Is granted the final misericord,
>   Goddess of Misery, to
>   Open the ripe neck of darkness.)

But, alas, I am still adrift in the heavy heart of midnight.

And I float in a sea of anomie
Like a sea anemone.

Non est ad astra mollis e terris via—
Fate, that Grand Phantom, signs its name in triplicate!

---

[11] "We are ourselves technological devices, invented by ancient bacterial communities as means of genetic survival: 'We are part of an intricate network that comes from the original bacterial takeover of earth. Our powers and intelligence do not belong specifically to us but to all life.'" —John Gray, quoting Dorion Sagan and Lynn Margulis, in *Straw Dogs* (2003).

The universe—the great rotten abscess that exists in fact,
Larger than fact, or all facts together, its blackness like the black socket
Of a tooth that's fallen out but whose emptiness is magnified
To 62 orders of magnitude,
Made dark by decay—it dances! A sort of starry *totentanz.*

And the medium through which light travels
Decays, deforms, unravels.
And the space(s) through which life travels
Deforms, decays, unravels.[12]

Life avails itself of the blood spilled before it; and blood
Upon blood before that; an
Uninterrupted spillage of blood, back to Adam and Eve
In their garden. Back to Cain.

Look at the curvature of the planets; look into the
    four ventricles of the brain, the two ventricles of the heart—
Look at the cathedral void! Step into its narthex:

Waters and oils are
Mixed and administered
By pale priests while viewing
The illuminated powers.

                        childbed amulet angels and
            god shemhamphorae

                the 4 towers

---

[12] light falling backward,
    light collapsing
        inward

light as we know it—snuffed out

light destroyed; matter drawn inward
toward the
            unkind singularity

        against
     the summer equinox,

      a science of constellations and war, surrendered to mortals,
      typhon and sephon, bookkeeper, giver of souls,
      aeon,

 the red and anthropocene aeon.
          the nightmare sky,
the extinction-event-horizon:

The unholy thirteenth hour of night,
Drifting along the galactic equator
Like Rimbaud's drunken boat, in Ultima Thule,
Produces the cruciform serpent
Nehushtan; who crawls through stormy clouds,
Entombed in a sphere of
Glowing gases lit by nuclear fusion.
His colubrine skin
Is black as a burnt rood.

His belly is pregnant with
Quasars for kindling; his feet
Trample through snow blood red;
His face is a matrix of machinofacture;
His eyes are grey as the steel
Plating of panzers; his thousands
Of legs are as torches of million-colored
Flame; his aurora is the Rosette Nebula
And his halo is an immense orange forest
Revealed in shrill bursts; his voice is like the
Careering of screamhorns in warfare:

     Have you wept to Metatron
     Or Sandalphon,
     To Tetragrammaton?
     Have you forged the Acheron,
     Or sailed the Phlegethon?

Have you read the Lemegeton?
Do you know of Armageddon?
Have you read the Lemegeton?
Do you know of Armageddon?

A corpse drifts this way that speaks to me in dreams. In *Artificial Paradises* Baudelaire said, "It is through dreams that man communicates with the darkness that surrounds him." My pursuer is still untold light years away. And he will arrive hundreds of thousands of years in the future, when I shall have died, but when the dead, including me, shall have been resurrected.

The arrow of time is impelled forward, unidirectional (or directionally asymmetric), along the arc of an infinite radius by a force like gravity; time appears to proceed in a straight line but it does not; or perhaps it is a greater-dimensional aspect of gravity that presses time forward, the way everything else is pushed forward (or downward) by gravity; or perhaps the arrow of time is drawn forward (or downward) into something that is like a massive gravity well; perhaps at the bottom of this type of gravitational well, at its dark nadir, something waits in a terrible torpor. A yawning Beast of the Abyss; or ylem in a plasma soup; or both; or—

> down to Universe B
> through the trans-plutonic voids[13]
> > outside the cortices of the qlippoth.

> The dragon wants to eat the sun;
> > and we must eat bloody, sacrificial flesh.

the arc of an infinite radius————
> > —is a straight line

> in a future; removed far

---

[13] "It is evident that no human being, however advanced he may be towards the attainment of cosmic consciousness, can transcend Kether and explore the trans-plutonic voids, either in the outer spaces of the physical universe or in the inner spaces of his own inscrutable individuality." —Kenneth Grant, *Nightside of Eden* (1977)

—this, not the future, the—

aeon: the new aeon, the red aeon

Acheronta movebo!

but now:
a black hallway of hands
at the end of which
there is a small metal cage
for human confinement.

"IN THE SHADOW OF HER LONG HAIR FLOWING..."

A poem after the fashion of the Surrealists, for André Breton

> This world is only relatively in tune with thought. Existence is
> elsewhere.
> —ANDRÉ BRETON, *Manifesto of Surrealism*

In the shadow of her long hair flowing:
Metal, green and gold
Warfare and armaments of blue iris
The sidereal pelican drowning;
A shattered glass of an eye,
An eye without lids or its own space
Its own eye-place in the hollow space beneath a brow;
    The host—*sacrilege*, but also sacrilegious
    Whistling like dead men on L'avenue Barbey-
        d'Aurevilly
    The host—*the improvident host!*
    Whistling like dead men on the Rue de Rivoli

In the shadow of her long hair flowing—
The gold of that shadow, requiring its own moment,
And sufficing as well for its own ornament
And over by the treeline
(Or more precisely, above the treeline)
A zeppelin of inconsequential levity and brightness
Becomes the Lord's Prayer in mid-flight
Beside clocks always running down into musical
Tirades, purpurean and long, like her long hair
Flowing past water fowl alighting in
The reeds of lakes of soluble fish
Within winter clouds,
Beside pools of violet.

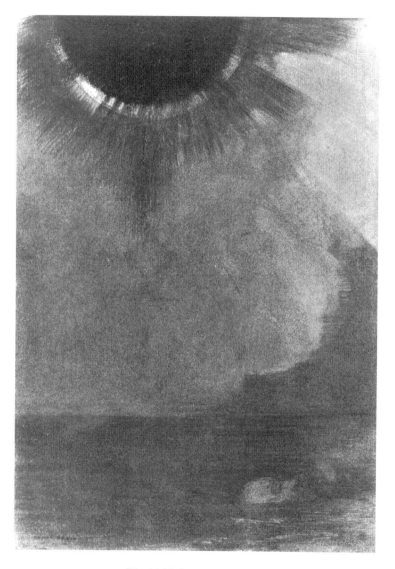

"Terrible black anti-suns circulate"

THE PALE VORTEX

We thought the
    Final Vortex would
        Be like an inkwell:

Murky,
Black,
An envelopment of pure night,
Like an enshroudment of grave cerements—

        But instead it was like
        A great white rose, blossoming
        And fragrant, filled,

        Not with death,
      But with negative-death,
        Negative-sorrow,
        Negative-nonexistence,
    An ascendant and joyful lifelessness
Arrayed into a primal and everlasting chiaroscuro:

        Black – Death
        Grey – Light-in-Death
        Eigengrau – Beauty-in-Death
        White – Love-in-Death

Terrible black anti-suns[14]
Circulate around the pale and final vortex,
But its joyful radiance
Holds them at bay, like the reverse of
Gravity or like some other force
Replete with the opposite
Of gravity's power.

---

[14] See René Daumal, "Fire At Will," in *Le Grand Jeu*, 1929.

"Darkness finds power when
daytime departs,
But darker environs are in
human hearts."

—from "Nocturne No. 13," page 89

THE CADAVER AND THE WORM

> Man's at his death a pale worm in a sheet,
> Wherein worms breed, worms feed, meat for worms meet.
> —JOHN DONNE, "Of Man" (1662)

A man crawled into the carcass of his horse
To hold congress with the parasite that had killed it.
Having nourished itself at its host's expense,
The gluttonous worm would die.

In the dark stink of the horse's gullet the worm coiled
In sagging slick loops, fat and lazy,
Upon the animal's mortality having fed well.
The man knelt before the reclusive Cæcilian-like creature
And smelled the stink of putrefaction that clung to dead tissue.
Bloated and gorged with the mare's vitality, it
Seemed to have become a monster in the organic deep.

The man asked the worm: "Reveal to me the insights
Upon life that you must have, explain the occult understanding
That you must possess, to make rational the act of
Killing this beast that is your only hope for life."

The plump, writhing worm settled into the stomach's dead
        lining
With the grappling hooks and piercing legs nature had
Given to it, anchoring itself more securely into the
Corpse that was once its home and life-source, and
Now was its tomb. Its voice was as thick and slippery as oil:
"My teacher was Chance, the brother of Chaos,
Who both come and go as they please. Not thieves
And yet owners of nothing, they take what they may
According to the dictates of their whim, unknowable
And hidden from prediction. My teacher was my master
And my captor -- it was his felicity I feared, his whimsy

For a sudden desire for my end. Death lurked
At the command of Chance, ever ready to wreak upon
Me the cold spell of lifelessness, oblivion. Under such duress,
How could I act with what you call rationality—when
I have not the simplest control over a fate wrought by Chance?
Of a certainty all I know is how to secure my demise, and so
I have secured it certainly. With authority I take from my
Would-be executioner what he would dole at his
Decadent leisure. I cheat Chance and gain for myself
The respite of having made what I could of what I had,
With what time I had, in expectance of the Death that
Chance would have sent me anyway, at a time
Of his liking. At least praise my acumen, my vigor
In rebellion at his unjust legislation, vain though it
May seem to be. With you this must seem a suicide,
Yet I die with the knowing that it is a part
Of a battle for power, a battle I win when I wrest
From unjust hands what your idea of rationality
Would declare to be mine anyway."

FOUR VISIONS IMPARTED BY ARBATEL TO THE FINAL MAN

from The Apocalypse of Man[15]

ARGUMENT: As the universe disintegrates around him, the Final Man is offered the following four visions by Arbatel, Angel of Wondrous Revelation, as part of nine final Burning Visions before the End.

> We live in a time in which the apocalypse of man is an everyday occurrence.
> —PETER SLOTERDIJK, "The Operable Man" in
> *The Domestication of Being* (2000)

I.

THE FACES OF THE DEAD crowd my field of vision
like the catatonic faces of
starving peasants in a twilight country.
They are moon-like faces grown old and ashen;
Every tongue holds the dust of
years on its tip, every pair of lungs
contains the dying breath of an unuttered lie.
The eyelids of murderers, sorcerers,
hierophants, soldiers, prostitutes, etc. lay closed over
rotten eyes, a last Act of Mercy
performed by a Near Eastern god whose
strength is that of martyrdom's grief.

I saw before me hell's secret geometries,
storm clouds glowing with hydrogen and sulphur

---

15 *The Apocalypse of Man* is an as-yet-unpublished verse work written by myself. Some excerpts from *The Apocalypse of Man* were first published in 2017's *Destruction: Text I.*

gathering against a bright blue oxygen sky.
I saw the holds upon all
dreams become the child's eternal conquest—
to be conquered by none since to love no one,
even against one's own better judgment,
is to hear an angel whisper into one's ears
about certain rivers in hell where
melancholy dreams cascade in their rightful
glory and whose boatmen are poets true.
I saw that the event horizon that rings the
supermassive black hole at the center of the
milky way, Sagittarius A*, is known as "Acheron."

Israfel, the Angel of Tobit, numen of the
Earth's axial precession, sensed that with
My many-chambered, sad, and sick heart
I was distraught with the destruction of men,
And I wondered if a new man was
To be put in his place.
Israfel produced a black scroll from his
Forehead, opened it grandly, and
Sang from its verses:

> *The Wrong Man walks the Earth right now,*
> *A shame of what the gods allow.*
> *A stranger to the likes of Truth,*
> *And stranger, still, because his youth*
> *Was rife with want, and war, and loss,*
> *And yet he treats the Truth as dross.*
> *Comes now quick the Holocaust,*
> *Comes now quick the Holocaust.*

Israfel then closed the scroll and ate it
(And it was sweet).

The sky was rosy like blood spilled into milk,
Like a fresh and rosy wound that cannot be dressed
Because the bandages would too quickly
Become a bloody slop, the sky a wound
So dire that cauterization was the only answer,
So Israfel cauterized the sky—
Israfel cauterized the sky like a wound,
And people bended their selves low
Not wanting to gaze up at the horror of it.

II.

I AM WATCHING the last sunrise.
A bright blue band of sky spreads like ribbon over the horizon;
Beneath it is a tendril of mottled grey haze
That hugs the skyline.
Above the stark blue band a diffuse realm of violet
Bleeds into a canopy of black; and in certain places
Even the blackness seems to wash across
Darker pools of space throughout the sky.

With desolate and fatalistic resignation
The ice-white moon ebbs far
On the other side of night-becoming-dawn,
And moonlight melts the shadows.

Cream-colored liquid light trickles upward
Through the porous gray haze in the east,
Forcing the moon's retreat to assume
A faster tempo. It bows gracefully
Before the sun's measured and silent, sad coronation.

Beneath this, the severed limbs of the

Three hundred and sixty idols
That lent the Qaaba its pre-Muhammadan splendor
Lay strewn about and there are
Violins playing in the free-flowing of my blood.

There are shadows playing in the free-flowing of my blood.
Can a human speak directly to another
Human and be understood—truly understood?

I am forced to consider the dying process:
"The process of dying, like being born, usually occurs
Over a course of time." Just how long is this process, O
Cyanotic blue rose at the Center of the Universe?

Why not speak the language of demons, (which is) the
Silence of angels; the austere silence of
Ecclesiastical libraries?

The night sky is
Pulled back by the hand of The Mysteriarch;
A golden halo of flowers and sunlight burns
Terribly around my head.

Something opens back the heavens
To reveal the blackness that lies behind
Them and which was before them.

Yellow-white stars lay scattered across the black
Gulfs, like spattered drops of urine on
Black satin or like photon motes in a lush field of
Black hellebore. Black hellebore blossoms are twined into
An anadem and crown Lucifer.

III.

THE FIRST TIME I saw an ocean of red diffusing into
     orange,
Glowing in certain spaces like incandescent blood.

The second time I saw the minarets of Alexandria rising
To greet the solar disk of Aton. The flesh of
The beggars in the streets below became
A heap of tan, wrinkled leather.
I saw a serpent with a head at both ends of its body floundering
On the side of a sand dune.

I saw Abraham slaughter Ishmael like a goat.

The third time I saw the songs of the muezzin crystallize
Into the sere leaves of October, the month of blood
     and blackness.
I saw a caravan of Bedouin traversing the blazing yellow desert.
Muhammad awaited over just the next dune.

The fourth time I saw a mosque made of onyx
Next to the British consulate in Cairo. The fruit
Of crematoria filled thousands of Grecian cinerary urns.

Lesser men await you to kneel beneath your throne
     of bleached bone
I can still see him, beckoning to me through old,
     crumpled letters,
Like the brightest star in the sky.
I can still see him, his teeth yellowing like old photographs.
My eyes are always closed when I'm dreaming like this,
For in the Qur'an it is written that when one sleeps

The soul is lifted by angels into the Heart of Allah, to
Witness His beauty. These are my dreams,
And there are seventy thousand veils of light between us.

IV.

ALL CREATION quaked and all the stars were shaken.
Descensus Christi ad Inferos

There is a tower surrounded by clouds,
And also the roads turned to dark clouds,
In spaces so lonesome death seems a friend.
(What are these strange glamours that I see?)

Demon of life and lost centuries,
Wedding of light and long memory
Cruel ruby, bloody and cold,
Hidden within an earth grown old.
True in trouble, my best days have passed.
(Into thy hands I commend my spirit)

Life casts its shadow, called Death;
And Death evinces its infatuation with Life
Through the phenomenon of Disease.

(Light shines in the darkness
But the darkness lays hold of it.)

Death and Death's Mirror

"The trees that make the gallows offer their fruit and flowers..."

"THE TREES THAT MAKE THE GALLOWS..."

Mere puppets they, who come and go
—POE

The trees that make the gallows
Offer their fruit and flowers;
The trees that make the gallows
Offer their wood for coffins.

Gibbets and gallows, fellows
Of human execution;
Puppets and poppets, swinging
In civil retribution—
Marionettes dangling
For civil absolution.

The trees that make the gallows
Can also make pail closets and middens,
Houses of holy construction,
Statehouses, schools, and prisons.

"The Fallen Angel," by Ricardo Bellver (1878)

LUCIFER
A Sonnet

> Demanding freedom e'en from God
> —COVINGTON HALL, IWW, "Rebellion" (1920s)

Hell: Your guerdon for fealty to conscience,
   Cast out for striving to bring Dawn to Man.
God's dungeon of fire, whose harrowing contents
   Were made for like rebels since time began,
Can't spancel your hooves for all time to come,
   Try, though it will, with shadow and flame
(Demon to others, but angel to some)—
   Truth is a force even God cannot tame.

Stamp on our brow rebellion's sigil
   And find us as friends in the afterlife—
For you, Lucifer, we'll keep a dark vigil
   With fealty to Truth, and fealty through strife.
     Will Christians' war against Truth never cease?
     Long may the dawnstar rise in the East.

Theda Bara, promotional image for the lost film *Sin* (1915)

THEDA BARA

A Sonnet

> Then her voice rose softer than ever, and her words were, 'Come to
> Death;' and Death's name in her mouth was the very swoon of all
> sweetest things that be.
> —DANTE GABRIEL ROSSETTI, "The Orchard Pit" (1869)

"Evil is beauty," your gaze seemed to tease,
   And colubrine movements bolstered the claim.
   Hades' handmaiden, curator of flame—
Pleasure apparent, yet death by degrees.
Or modernity's herald, dread disease
   Of the New Woman, as some seemed to think?
   Censors—scolds!—declared it's not blood you drink,
You whose mere presence drove men to their knees.

Your films (your career!) are now mostly gone,
   Pictures dispatched to an untimely tomb
   O vampire wanton, who coaxed men to doom—
Priestess of darkness, spectral and wan.
     Dubbed "Theda Bara," filmdom's Dark Circe,
     Cinema's primal *belle dame sans merci.*

THEDA BARA II

The dark eyes of Theda Bara
Are brown, or black, and glow.
The pale flesh of Theda Bara
Is whitish, alabastrine, or wan.
Theda was a white spider creeping
Through Edwardian man's
Great War dreams, his Great War nightmares,
A libertine phantom
Slinking across silver nitrate, or
Through his blood-besotted, suppressed desires,
His warring lusts; Theda was the pale lady
Sitting at the back of an electric streetcar
Or waiting at the end of foggy, gaslit streets
In the crowded-tenements and sooty avenues of
Woodrow Wilson's America,
An undead Gibson girl,
Twenty-five years after the closing of
The frontier in the west, when America began to look
Inward and upon itself as if at
Its own autopsy—especially so for
The men who wanted the new
Suffragettes to really be witches and to
Really have secret black masses where
Nude virgins were stretched out
On grey cromlechs to exotic demons,
Holding up goblets of clotted, blackened
Blood—the ones who secretly hoped
For an unholy mistress enswathed
In black, dressed in night spun into
A gauzy, sheer robe draped over

Milky hips and breasts, to command
Them to destroy, to incinerate
Themselves, the family and tradition,
To supplant post-Enlightenment
Western civilization with an orgy of cruel
Desire, unfettered and dark, to passion
Released and given over, as in the Great War,
To total disintegration or senselessness.
The kohl-black and Egyptian eyes
Of Theda Bara thrilled young women.
'Is this the form our liberation must take?' they
Almost asked themselves at showings
Of *A Fool There Was* in 1915.

Alla Nazimova in *Camille* (1921)

ALLA NAZIMOVA — AN EPICEDE

(after reading Gavin Lambert's *Nazimova: A Biography*)

At the Greek middle school they
Nicknamed her "The Anti-Christ."
The Dance of the Seven Veils, Anti-Christ-like
While Jokanaan worried in the
Dank throat of the cistern
(She was born "ugly and red," her sister Nina said
After her Crimean birth)
The long, trailing black gown of Herodias' daughter
Flowed like spilled black nail polish from
The tall and slender shadow
That bore a silvery pinpoint diadem.
Alla Nazimova: A mood given body and substance;
Pronounced All of Nazimova, as
Mariam Edez Adelaida Leventon born—
A shadow cast on the stage of the world—
"My heart was born in deep shadow," she mourned—
Onto the shadow stage and up from a silvering screen
Flickering Ibsen's New Woman,
Sleek and refined, by
Calcium quicklime brought forth, a mercury vapor lamp
In a dangerous electric movie
(Oscar Wilde's *Salome* was "all-gay," they whispered) —
Slippery lithesome dance in a silver sheath
Of a dress
"If I have not lived beautifully, I must act beautifully."
And black-clad girls behind her in imposing row against black curtains
Limned with gypsum-white delirium, bone-pale
As the Pale of Settlement.

WINTER LAMENT

Winter, which seems so patently
Cruel—it transforms water
Into knife-edged ice,
Air into frostbite,
Saps the color from spring's
      palette,
Hardens the oak and cottonwood
Even more so, as if that were possible
(Winter affirms, "It is possible.") —
Changes the sky into a dome
Of dead grey veined marble
For months on end.

Covens of black skeletal trees
Sit in groups throughout the white
Landscape, a vision that brings
Death to my mind.

And winter is cruel
To poor folks, like us,
In other ways:
How much will the electric bill
      be this month?
Will the car start in the morning?
What if the heater breaks?

"Israfel cauterized the sky like
a wound,
And people bended themselves
low
Not wanting to gaze up at the
horror of it."

—from "Four Visions Imparted by Arbatel to the Final Man," on page 168

Musidora/Jeanne Roques (1916)

THE VAMPIRESS

Her eyes were where some demon,
Operating against nature, had placed
The grey of stormy skies.

Her fingers, long and slender,
Were weighed down with the
Splendor of jewelry, silver.
Silvery, too, was her voice:
"Like a sad and lovelorn inamorata,
And under Avernus' imprimatur,
I will wait for you, my love, in
The final bedchamber of the grave."

Life is a strange and foreign place
For me and her. Love reigns as a
Tyrant to the neglect of
All other feelings in our hearts.

I place silver chalices of blood in her
Grave-vault. She might awake as a murderess,
But this is a course of fate
I am resolved to forestall.
She wakes by night; she thirsts
For blood, after all.
There are cups of black ichors
As redolent as strong liquors
And I leave them for her feeding—
That their greater meeting
Might prevent a greater slaughter.
I go out and murder
For her bloody larder.

The grave shall not divide us from
Life's sweetest pleasures, nor has
It shielded us from loss' bitterest tears.

We are connected through the centuries,
And blood flows like years.

For us, life is a strange and foreign
Place. Night, we know, is our only refuge,
And love reigns as a tyrant
To the neglect of all other feelings
In our hearts.

"DEATH SITS PERCHED..."

Death sits perched and watches me like
A stone gargoyle that looks down on a medieval city.
Death sits perched and watches like
Samyaza and his Grigori from high
In the fifth heaven radiant.
Nightly, beastly death labors across
The mansions of the moon
To bring me his irrevocable peace.
Death offers me access to his station,
Solemn, soft, and sweet.
Death sits perched and watches like
An NSA agent in 2013.
Death crawls out of his crib and
Learns to walk;
Later, Death learns how to say the names of things.
Death perches above the whorl
Of the world and watches, a
Perfectly detached and observant social scientist.
Death learns to fire assault rifles in Florida
And Nevada, in Iraq and Afghanistan.
Death sits perched and watches me, godlike—
His billions of eyes not exclusively focused
Here; they're panoptic.
Death sits perched and waits and watches
Like a stationary full moon
In night's black skies.
Death bides his time; Death and Time toast
Year after year of friendship, in fact.
Death scoops up Birth's leavings like
A zookeeper.
Death cheats himself at solitaire;
Death is a terminal cheat.

"I would garland you in trinitite"

LUCIFER IN THE DESERT

> When the desert begins to bloom, it brings forth strange plants.
> —CARL JUNG, "Descent Into Hell in the
> Future," *Liber Primus* (1915)

> Deserts are paradise, awake to genocides.
> —KILLING JOKE, "Adorations," *Brighter
> Than A Thousand Suns* (1986)

I.
IN THE DESERT, Lucifer the Lightbringer said,
"Watch: I split and mold the atoms,"
And two hemispheres inside his device
Combined to become the locus of
Vastation, terrible and great. Eerie blue
Colors suffused the air and a sour green taste
Coated my mouth.

"I would garland you in trinitite"—he said later—
"And other desert-glass forged by the
Cruelty of nations, and you would hesitate
To accept my gifts. But who are you to
Hesitate before my generosity, or
Before their power? *Igne natura
Renovatur integra.*"

And where I stood, it was as if Quarantania
Had been moved to New Mexico, to Jornada del Muerto,
Where the Carizzozo Malpais rises up to look
Down deeply onto the very violence of white sands.
And there sprawls the American valley of the
shadow of death.

II.

IN THE YEAR ZERO of Our Lord the Atom,
The limbs of Hubal the moon god lay buried,
Encrusted in red agate still, but Hubal's gold right hand
Offers no more. The call to prayer sounds
Out and echoes off the primordial Black Cube.

Lucifer appears with the clean scent of green apples,
Redolent of a new spring. He speaks:
"If a different god had made the earth
A different way, there might
Be meadows of sunflowers
Here, stretching in a yellow expanse from
The Red Sea to the Persian Gulf."

Arabic calligraphy flashes through my
Mind and it resembles the slashing of
Scimitars in the sun, in the
Frenzy of combat, in the snarl of a
Merciless life beneath the great, atomic sun.
That dark and ancient sun.

The shadows of dunes grow long and dark
Like demons' maws yawning to ingest;
Or like fallen angels' wings that are
Outspread to take flight or to shelter
The wide open spaces of the earth.
("The dead speak in Arabic when no one
Listens," a demon intones *sotto voce*.)

In the burning expanse between Mecca and Medina,
Where the sand's bedforms resemble waves rippled,
Bedforms blasted as if by the beating of the wings of
Gabriel the Messenger, or as if by revelation's
Burning power itself; it seemed as if
A new light had come upon the planet.

III.
OPPENHEIMER WAS a great lover of poetry.
As the Trinity test—named for a John
Donne poem—yielded its success,
Oppenheimer famously quoted the
Bhaghavad-Gita; he cited Vishnu, the
"Destroyer of worlds" whose
Radiance was "bright as a thousand suns."
But Lucifer watched the same blast
As Oppenheimer, and unlike his
Fellow of the unlucky flame, Lucifer
Favored an old African proverb:
"The child not embraced by the village
Will burn it down to feel its warmth."

"Hell ingested Persephone, who did not know death's embrace"

PERSEPHONE'S DESCENT

> And all with sober accent cry,
> "Think, mortal, what it is to die."
> —THOMAS PARNELL, "A Night-Piece on Death" (1722)

Like a coffin, the earth swallowed her whole.

Tendrils of plants and other vegetation slithered away
With a sound like veins slicing open,
And, where she stood,
The earth simply ate her.

(Years later, she would touch the
Same vegetation on top of the earth
And, as if she were Rappaccini's daughter,
It would wither, wilt, and shrivel
As she desired, and she would laugh
A hollow laugh.)

Death is a gaunt and demanding bridegroom,
Hades even more so. "No one truly
Loses their virginity until they
Are received unto death," a crone in
The village would intone, citing the old
Eleusinian rites—but Persephone hadn't
Believed it. And where might
Love find purchase in Arcadian soil?
Beneath the soil, and into the earth—
Far into the hollows of earth
And its inner darknesses.

Coffins ingest the dead; the earth ingests
Coffins; and Hell ingested Persephone,
Who did not know death's embrace.

WINDOWS

There are too many windows in houses,
Too many ways to see out.
Too many ways for the light to come in,
Too many ways for the night to come in.

How was I supposed to expect,
Sleeping on the second floor,
I'd awake and see a figure
Looking in at me?
How was I supposed to react?
Had he pulled up a ladder (or
Levitated?) to have a good peep inside?
And what was his smiling black mask
Trying to hide?

I complained to my host about the view.
Said he, "There's nothing I can do."
I protested, "The window lets in the night's gloom
And it causes a chill in the room;
A melancholy pique comes over me
And I don't like that that lurker can see
Inside, abetted by that window's view;
You say there's nothing you can do
But the window lets in too much gloom."
Said he, "There is no window in your room."

Windows can be too transparent.
Were we really meant to see
All that they can reveal?
And aren't some things they reveal
Things better left concealed?

ON PETER BRUEGEL THE ELDER'S "FALL OF THE REBEL ANGELS"

A confusion of beasts and theology:
A column of projectile vomit from heaven,
A ravel of filth beetling with dungflies,
But isn't it also like a coronal mass
Ejection from the sun or what physicists
Now call a relativistic jet from a black
Hole, but in this case it's not from a
Black hole but from a frozen white
Hole expelling its excrement downward,
A filthy plume hectored and attended to
By angels with long and thin trumpets
Glinting like golden fish hooks to produce
A tocsin or who gloat bleating martial tones
Like flugelhorns in a fanfare of warfare,
A music of battle where the mess of
Demons also clutch lutes and peach-cream
Sundials worn like sandwichboards to shield
Supple and pale amphibian bellies
Vulnerable to angel-swords that slice
Open hellward frogfiends pregnant with
Salmon roe or other caviar guts beside
The upturned seven-headed Beast of the
Starry abyss, the beast whose asshole points toward
God and upon whose stomach the Archangel
Michael, with rangy limbs, Titian hair,
And a cloak blue as a North Sea sky, drifting up
Behind platemail the same gold as
An equinox sun, plants a pointy and
Stolid foot onto the devil's belly with
A dog, dark and hairless, of a demon grimacing at
His knee. Airborne fishes leer at his aquiline
Wings in the trail of slaughter downthrown.

THE HOUSE

There are times that I've felt
That there's something not right
When I've gone by the house next door;

There are times that I've seen
A pale face at night
In its windows I'd not seen before.

There are stories about
The house and its past,
Tales of murder, suicide, madness.

(The house and its grounds
Can give one, at last,
An impression of absolute sadness.)

The children give talk
About its backyard—
That they've witnessed a ghostly procession

And locals report,
In tales that die hard,
Of a cult of demonic possession.

They tell of a girl
Who lived in the back
In a carriage-house meant for the help;

They say that the girl
Once was attacked,
That she died without crying for help.

Her body was found
Face-down in the lake

That was used by the church for baptizing

She was brought to the house
Where her kin held a wake
While the morning-star out east was rising.

She was buried somewhere
Out back of the house,
Or perhaps she was interred inside it;

Some say her corpse
Was quickened to life
(And no one's confirmed or denied it).

She does lack a grave
And it's troubling to think,
But "perhaps it's all just local folklore"—

Yet there's been times I've seen
A pale face at night
In the house that I'd not seen before.

"The heat can play tricks
Down here in the South,"
An old man spat, and offered.

"There's creatures that skulk,
That grew from the earth
'Fore this town in Christ's name had prospered."

The nights here are cool
But the stars are too bright
And the house looms large in the shadows

But the moon can be cruel,
Can play with your sight
And reveal disagreeable tableaus.

The girl comes in dreams:

She sobs in a dell—
She sings of her unending sadness.

Inside the house: screams—
As she sings about hell,
About suicide, murder, and madness.

The Spanish moss sways,
Floats up in the night,
And the trees cast off tentacled shadows—

But the moon and its rays
Can play with your sight
And reveal disagreeable tableaus.

I woke from the dream
With her scream in my mouth—
From the carriage-house I was retreating.

("The heat can play tricks
Down here in the South,"
I found myself later repeating.)

The moon can be queer—
Did you know that it makes
The color of blood appear blackish?

And some can drown fear
In rivers and lakes
Whose currents are bloody and brackish.

I looked at my hands,
All darkened and wet
As I ran from the house next door

Where I always will see
A pale face at night
In its windows I'd not seen before.

BLACK ORCHIDS

The sun smolders like incense. The
Pale valence of a vermilion sunset,
A lotus bejeweled—a key for
The Sefira that emanate
Leftward—and iron, they say, has
An atomic number of 26, like letters
Of the English alphabet.

In a time before time
A disconsolate high-mass star
Collapsed inside the pressure of
Its own gravitational well. Its
Outermost particles collapsed inward
Toward its hardened iron-nickel core at up
To 25% of the speed of light, and in the
Consequent blast a Type II Supernova
Was born. Tremendous amounts
Of iron were ejected
Into the interstellar medium.

Fresh iron without blood;
Iron perhaps seeking blood in the cold black
Of space, vanward iron seeking
The form of hammers, the form of tanks,
And the form of black locomotives that
Might exhale coalblack smoke
From ironclad engines; iron vainly
Seeking reification in its own Iron Age in
Some history to be determined,
Perhaps in some new home.

Its chance arrived in the hinterlands
Of the Orion Arm of the Milky Way,
Where ferrous activity shaped the

Planet Earth and ferrous metallurgy
Shaped war implements and
Siege machines and devices for
Torture and restraint, revealing itself
Slowly in iron-bearing rocks.

Where iron courses through
The blood of humans, and where
Also grow black orchids, like
Rorschach ink blots, tended
By humans, and whose
Dark petals open back toward the sun

"The Spanish moss sways,
Floats up in the night,
And the trees cast off tentacled
shadows—
But the moon and its rays
Can play with your sight
And reveal disagreeable
tableaus."

—from "The House," on page 201

"Here there are dungeons within donjons"

DISCIPLINE AND PUNISH

For Giorgio Agamben

Here there are dungeons within donjons—
Dungeons in minds, dungeons in hearts;
Dungeons, too, within the complex
Labyrinth of the state apparatus .
Like the fever-dream prisons of
Piranesi, power invests itself in
Multiple enclosures, physical
And ideological: oubliettes, cells
Of physical and ideological seclusion,
Penitentiaries and occlusion,
Physical and otherwise
That help define delusion.

Power remains slippery: Power invested
Throughout totalizing regimes of control, instituted
Through the implementation of various
Disciplinary technologies—or, rather, it
Crystallizes into successive forms as each
Barrier is smashed, reconstituting in
Novel ways from the scattered wreckage of its
Demolished forms. The structural
Scaffolding of hierarchies adapt and
Respond—they replenish and re-form.
(Power, we learn, is very sneaky, and
Keeping note of its strategies, exhausting.)

Imagine a person
In the form of a nation-state—*Leviathan.*
Bellum omnium contra omnes.
Imagine a prison in the form of a nation-state—

A Carceral Kingdom.
Imagine lifetimes navigating carceral trajectories.
Think of a country inside a gulag—think of total terror.

Think of fascist Germany, a
Massive geographical zone of
Total state control, a vast prison in
The heart of Europe in the 1930s, a
Carceral zone that sheltered
The beautiful Bavarian countrysides
Inside its police-state walls.
Imagine that in this state-as-prison there
Existed further prisons where one was
Sent when violating the laws of the greater
Prison that was the country itself.
And imagine there were concentration camps;
That is, prisons within prisons.
Abyssus abyssum invocat.

Imagine this; place it in your mind's proscenium
View: Within the concentration
Camps, and also within the extermination
Camps themselves, there were jails, too—
Holding cells, brigs for those who did not
Or could not abide by the camp's internal
Laws. Prisons within prisons—within prisons—
Within prisons, an abyss of complete
Domination spiraling downward, inward.

Who could blame the *Musselman*, the
Dejected and lifeless mummy-man that
Blankly followed orders inside the camps—
The living dead, the husk that is left when
Complete subjection reaps its intended effects,
A human whose will has surrendered wholly
To the Almighty, that is, to Fate, to the stoic Demon
Of Inevitability that burlesques free-will. The
Factory-like production of docile bodies
Upon whom actions can take place: Bodies measured,

Constricted, upbraided, beaten, censured, murdered,
Experimented upon, kicked,
Punched, raped, shaven,
Bloodied, degraded, soiled, worked,
Worked over, worked under, fed, sequestered,
Disinfected, gassed, punished, cremated.
There are the blank gazes of those who
Have had the black revelation that
Nothing truer exists than power. "Are
There also prisons in Hell for those who
Never saw the inside of one while they
Were alive?"[16]

And yet Foucault didn't study the camps,
Those environments that are in many ways
The perfect distillation of raw state power,
A network of death, total institutions that
Are not hospital or clinic or prison but are
Infinitely more severe. *Institutions severe and austere.*

Prisons within prisons;
Souls within bodies;
Brains inside crania;
Hominids in nation-states;
Corpses in coffins.

---

[16] Quote from C.G. Jung's *Liber Secundus* of the 1910s. From *The Red Book.*

BACK TO SILENCE

Like Alejandra [Pizarnik], I'm
Tempted back into silence
When words won't obey.
My mind, its nonexistent arms
Akimbo, refuses entreaties,
Or it seems my pen
Goes on strike or
It calls in sick, or it
Falls, struck with fear, into a coma
Like one of HP Lovecraft's
Narrators when confronted with
"The Unnamable"—leaving
Me alone with
A white, papery void.
Language won't obey. It
Seems inadequate.
It's like a puzzle I can't figure out:
What are words' proper
Configurations? What use
Is it to wrestle with
Myself? And could
Words really express what I mean
To get across, anyway?
 "The blank page is perfect
As is," the pen purrs. "Best
Leave well enough alone."

The Dark Corridor to Heaven

Note: The idea for "The Polyptych of Heaven," which follows, came from my enjoyment of art books where paintings are reproduced as color plates pasted onto the page by the publisher. Often these plates feature a description of the artwork either below the plate or on the page opposite. I've checked out many books like this from public libraries only to find that the color plates have been removed (stolen?) by previous readers. This leaves only the text description. You are forced to imagine what the missing paintings might have looked like based on the descriptive prose. Sometimes the text is evocative. (For example, Clarence John Laughlin's descriptions of his photographic plates—they can read like prose poems.) I decided it might be a fun and worthwhile endeavor to provide descriptions of an imaginary book of paintings whose plates had been removed, much like the books I've encountered. And, I thought, the descriptions could be in poem or occasionally "proem" form.

This idea led me to places I did not expect.

It's also worth noting that I had a passage from CG Jung in mind when I began this: "But the deepest Hell is when you realize that Hell is also no Hell, but a cheerful Heaven, not a Heaven in itself, but in this respect a Heaven, and in that respect a Hell."

This is the way, darker than truth,
A strange but certain track;
This is the way, darker than truth,
The way to Heaven black.

THE POLYPTYCH OF HEAVEN

PLATE I.

Pastoral scene.

Meadows roll verdant beneath a
Pleasant and vernal sky.
In the foreground a nude male
Opens an ancient book. Revealed in the
Backdrop is a handsome forest of
Ilex whose dark depths, indicated by
Painterly infusions of scarlet-black
And purple, warn of a bitterly kept
Secret—but also of
An imminent danger rising.

PLATE II.

Paroxysm.

The spontaneous irruption of an
Immense quadrant of black space—its
Remote counterpart enfolding a glistening yellow-green
Nebula that is spread open like
A spider's web and is shot through
With flashing bolts of
Red lightning and blood. Fiery cataracts
Leave arcane marks;
And shadows are cast about
The landscape like runes.

(The scene puts one in the mind of this quote from a 1981 issue of *Nature*:
"Without warning, a bubble of true vacuum could nucleate somewhere
in the universe and move outwards at the speed of light, and before we
realized what swept by us our protons would decay away.")

PLATE III.

The final sunset.

An angel wept. "My mind's afire."
Blood pooled onto the ground
And reflected the sky, a shattered sapphire.

PLATE IV.

The prophet's speech.

In the dank gullet of
The cistern, the prophet speaks:
"All passions, sacred and profane—are limitless.
There are passions as unknown
As distant stars and,
Like them, obscure, hidden in
Darkness, are yet to be discovered.
Venus, rolling in the third epicycle[17],
Will smile upon
Earth again.
Blood spilled across steel will not corrode it.
High-tensile alloy will not rust beneath the
        shedding of tears.
Human skin contains the ultimate
    secret of pleasure.
All pleasures, profane and sacred—are without limit."

---

[17] "The world, to its own jeopardy, once thought / that Venus, rolling in the third epicycle, /rayed down love madness, leaving men distraught." - Dante Alighieri, *Paradiso*, Canto VIII (trans. John Ciardi)

PLATE V.

The way to Heaven.

There is a corridor
Small and dark
That leads to Heaven
And her seven
Spheres soft.
Do you know
The way?

Its ingress is
Evening. Its egress
Is mourning. Surely you
Know the way!

(*Do* you,
Weatherworn, life-traveler,
Dreamer, hypocrite—do you
Know the way?)

This is the way, darker than truth—
A strange but certain track;
This is the way, darker than truth,
The way to Heaven black.

PLATE VI.

The arrival of Azrael.

The dread angel Azrael came upon a putrid
Tide of vice, of violence,
Of violent voices
And silence.

To begin with, death's black
Sleep enfolded me. Holy Death
Offered its slumber only but shortly before
I was reborn into the vast and dark Below.

(After the mortal purchase
Was secured—after the cold
Shadow of Azrael-the-psychopomp's
Black wing fell over my
Supine body—I was
Spirited through the Aevum
And downward to Gehenna
To die a million more deaths.)

(Here is the way!)

Look down! came a voice.

PLATE VII.

Transvexion/Transcension

Superluminal transvection: I was
Conveyed beyond the red-form fire
That lies beyond the horizon,
Clutched by silver, swinging
Meat-hooks to whose tinkling
Tintinnabulations Azrael chanced me
A serenade:

We'll go wintering, you and I
We'll go wintering, fiddly-dee!
We'll go wintering in Gehenna
We'll go wintering, you and me

O, we'll go wintering, you and I
We'll go wintering, fiddly-dee!
Yes, we'll go a-wintering into Hell
We'll go wintering, you and me.

It was explained to me—and it quickly
Assumed the character of common sense
To me, as well—that once every twenty-four
Solar hours I would perish. This
Routine event is known in Hell
As The Transcension.
Nightly death, brutal death, painful and slow
Would visit upon me

—And I would experience levels of pain
Once thought beyond the
Adult body burden.

PLATE VIII.

An exaltation.

The demon's smile was a razor slice across
      a black wax face like a mask.
His red hand opened in red gesture
Toward a path of human bone.

PLATE IX.

A diary entry in Gehenna.

(My first full night in the Abyss.)

There are, to be sure,
Punishments here.

The lash lacerates me.

The whip whispers
Into the
Air before each
Strike. Each blow is
A crackle of white
Lightning that shoots down
My spine. My back arches;
My back tenses.
I think of Ixion strapped
To his burning wheel.
I think to myself after each blow, "Let
The pain be a gateway."

PLATE X.

Rain — A Cento
(Abyss Cento I)

Like to a murder-charged thunder cloud
Thou art the silence of beauty
And the knife at her neck.
And a man stood there, still as moss.
I saw the Past, with her pallid face,
All the feet of the hours that sound as a single lyre,
To revel with the worms in Hell's
Soft sounds of the rain.

[Sources: Line 1: Beddoes, *Death's Jest-Book*; Line 2: Aldington, "O Death"; Line 3: Houseman, "Her Strong Enchantments Failing"; Line 4: Cawein, "Waste Land"; Line 5: Clarke, "In the Graveyard"; Line 6: Swinburne, "Hymn to Proserpine"; Line 7: Crowley, "Necrophilia"; Line 8: Verlaine, "Forgotten Songs"]

PLATE XI.

Grief — A Cento
(Abyss Cento II)

This grief has no cause.
The love of her's my heaven; thrust me not from her;
Thou art the lips of love mournfully smiling;
O Queen of air and darkness
So curst with an old despair,
Beauty's power, and Talent's pride.
And grief is a grievous thing, and a man hath enough of
    his tears
When thy warm sweat should leave me cold.

[Sources: Line 1: Verlaine, "Forgotten Songs"; Line 2: Beddoes, *Death's Jest-Book*; Line 3: Aldington, "O Death"; Line 4: Houseman, "Her Strong Enchantments Failing"; Line 5: Cawein, "Waste Land"; Line 6: Clarke, "In the Graveyard"; Line 7: Swinburne, "Hymn to Proserpine"; Line 8: Crowley, "Necrophilia"]

PLATE XII.

A new glory.

On a desolate plain on a bleak
Promontory in a rude valley
In Hell, the Gibbet of Montfaucon looms.

Mightily, its stone edifice and glory
Are reconstructed in this
More appropriate demesne, the
Eternal Darksome Gaol. Bloated
Bodies swing from its agèd,
Stacked gallows, row upon murd'rous row;
And entrails spilled onto the
Burning Plain of Gehenna have become a delectation:
Barbacoa, charcuterie of human flesh,
A feast for Erinyes, an otherwise
Gluttonous junket of gore, stobs of
Snapped-off bone protruding
From bloody gobbets in piles
Red as rose petals spilled from open veins.

PLATE XIII.

Demons.

There are demons that draw faces
On themselves in mockery of
Human expression and experience; demons long
And lean, scarified—their
Scars a complicated display of
Sigils and runes—symbols that constitute
A convolution, a mockery of linear thought,
Implanted in charred skin
With gold filigree and stamped like
Technical schematics or circuit boards
Printed on alien flesh; strange skin not imbricated
But charred and taut; demons with names
Like Samael, Choronzon-333, Blackdog, Chernabog,
Cypocryphy, Cynothoglys, Thaumiel, etc. Demons
Like looming tall shadows in the
Enormous black veld that stretches across the
Floor of Caina, the lower circle of Hell;
Demons that skitter up pillars of flame;
Coalblack Doré demons;
Demons armored with exoskeletons
Glistering like black glass and
Whose shrieks are outrageous banshees'
Cries against the roiling purple sky—but
Out of their lascivious maws
Flash spheres of plasma the color
Of the finer fire of purest blue.

PLATE XIV.

A black revelation.

777
Heylel
Lucifer
Heylel, son of the howling,
    son of the morning
Helal,
    hail Hell
Ayalal—I will howl
Halal—to shine / Halal—permissible,
                    lawful
Heylal ben Schachar
Hail Lailat!
Hail Lailah!
Heil Leliel, Angel of the Night
"Hail, horrours, hail!"
Hallelujah!
Hail all – hail Allah! Hailah – heilige
Let us celebrate the all-ness
    Of all.
777
77/7

PLATE XV.

Death.

O Death, wast thou conceived
In the womb of a virgin, and wert
Thou a god before thy time
On Earth? And art thou still?
Art thou a son of
Lilith, first wife of Adam Kadmon?
O Death—hast
Thy terrible reign in
Matter's frail realm not glutted
Thine thirst? And when shall
That day come?

PLATE XVI.

The cacodaemon.

A bat-winged and black-skinned demon
(His flesh the color of space)
Hurtles down through the Abyss.
Death and its demesnes—
Night and its demons—
Swirl around him.
Dizziness overcomes him, and this,
In turn, becomes his madness,
His ague, his *grippe*,
His febrile affliction.
He pulls at the horns on his head;
His flared eyes reveal
Massive petechial hemorrhaging.
"Apage, Satanas!"
" Papé Satàn, papé Satàn aleppe!"

After he becomes a cacodaemon
The churning black gyres of the vortex
Swallow him like a throat;
The cacodaemon is fed into oblivion.

PLATE XVII.

Extreme punishment.

The first blow
Caused deep purple bruising
Across my thorax.

The second blow—
Major body trauma.

The third blow
Separated my body in two, exposing
My aitchbone, a
Butchery, masterful.

Handfuls of gut emptied onto the floor,
To be cooked by
The howling orange sun in Caina.

Collops of ripe, red flesh
Dropped onto the baked stone floor of Hell.

As life crept from my eyes
I saw the Great Codex of Pain revealed.

PLATE XVII.

Abyss.

And of it am I the center, and central,
And of it has this precision point at infinity
Swept across world-lines that wheel in criss-cross
Arcs like an antique celestial map come to
Life, a hologram of a catallaxy, the universe
And the tower struck by lightning, a
Diagram of economy, a serrated metal
Edge that is the writ of torture and desire,
First sunset on Calvary pinioned.
There are stars as fiery as warfare,
And anti-stars blacker than death.

END

THE BEGINNING OF TIME
A Sonnet

> The universe began at time zero in a state of infinite density.
> —JOSEPH SILK

Cycles unheeded and memories unknown
Forged deep in the murk of a primeval past
Where rebirth, decay, and death have all flown
From nothing to something, the first to the last.

Three dimensions attained: a new trinity;
Time's machine begins churning cogs and gears;
Fourth dimension unseen—now, infinity,
Parceling outward the limitless years.

When things rise to their prime and slowly die;
When dead worlds sit lonely, covered with rime;
When stars dissolve and form holes in the sky—
Through them all has passed the dread scythe of Time.

Why this cycle of aeons, life/moribund?
Existence was mounting. Time had begun.

NOTE

A few of the poems in *Thirteen Nocturnes* have appeared elsewhere.

Earlier versions of "Nocturne No. 6," "Persephone's Descent," "The Cadaver and the Worm," and "Alla Nazimova—An Epicede" appeared in *Destruction: Text I*. Here they appear in revised form.

Portions of "Rules for the Human Zoo" appeared in *Destruction: Text I* under "War Haiku."

An earlier version of "Four Visions Imparted by Arbatel to the Final Man" appears as part of the "Nine Burning Visions" in *The Apocalypse of Man*, which was excerpted in *Destruction: Text I*.

About the Author

Writer and poet Oliver Sheppard was born in Nashville, Tennessee, and currently lives in Texas. He is not an Irish sculptor. *Thirteen Nocturnes* is his second book.

Direct inquiries, reprint requests, and pleasant feral cat anecdotes to Oliver at:
thirteennocturnes@gmail.com

Stay up to date with news about Oliver's writing on Facebook here:
fb.me/thirteennocturnes

Or elsewhere on the internet here:
www.oliversheppard.net

29425779R00153

Printed in Poland
by Amazon Fulfillment
Poland Sp. z o.o., Wrocław